SHE
THINKS

THE ***ENTREPRENEURIAL WOMAN'S*** GUIDE
TO MOVING PAST THE ***MESSY MIDDLE***
AND INTO ***THE EXTRAORDINARY***

SHE
THINKS

THE *ENTREPRENEURIAL WOMAN'S* GUIDE TO MOVING PAST THE *MESSY MIDDLE* AND INTO *THE EXTRAORDINARY*

ANDREA LIEBROSS

Niche Pressworks

SHE THINKS BIG: *The Entrepreneurial Woman's Guide to Moving Past the Messy Middle and into the Extraordinary*

ISBN-13:   978-1-952654-82-4 Hardback
            978-1-952654-83-1 Paperback
            978-1-952654-84-8 eBook

Library of Congress Cataloging-in-Publication Data on File at lccn.loc.gov

For permission to reprint portions of this content or bulk purchases, contact support@AndreaLiebross.com.

Published by Niche Pressworks; http://NichePressworks.com
Indianapolis, IN

The views expressed herein are solely those of the author and do not necessarily reflect the views of the publisher.

WHAT OTHERS ARE SAYING

This is a brave and compelling book. Andrea's lessons are ambitiously changing the narrative of what it means to be a woman, mom, daughter, and friend while becoming a successful entrepreneur.
— **MEGAN HYATT MILLER,** president and CEO, Full Focus

Andrea Liebross is vulnerable, honest, and real. Oh, and a total badass. If you've ever struggled with feeling unfulfilled on your journey as a female entrepreneur, you will see yourself in this book. But the best part? Andrea will show you exactly how to identify what's holding you back so you can elevate your entire life to the next level.
— **NIKKI ODEN,** author of *But Definitely Wear Mascara*

Andrea doesn't hold back. She asks thought-provoking questions that get us to look at ourselves differently, question each thought, and change long-held perspectives about ourselves and our businesses. The result? Resilient confidence that serves us for the rest of our lives. If you read only one entrepreneurship book this year, make it this one!
— **KATE GREUNKE,** CEO, Socialite Agency

If you are a successful entrepreneur but have even an inkling that there is another level of success and you are meant for more, this book is for you. Andrea gives you the permission to want more, be more, and achieve more, and she gives you the tools to bring it into your reality in a way that works for your life.
— **STACEY HYLEN,** coach and author of *Hidden Profits*

Andrea is brilliantly relatable, and each page feels like it was written just for me! Filled with practical advice and wisdom, this is a must-read for any female entrepreneur who feels stuck and wants to be happier in work and life.

— **JILL TIRONE,** dance studio consultant and web designer

Get ready to take notes! There are so many useful nuggets in this book. Andrea has a great way of intuiting situations that any business owner and woman can relate to. *She Thinks Big* will help you figure out how to move past your own blocks. The book lays out clear steps you can take to shift your mindset away from fear and into your next version of success, regardless of where you are starting. You need this excellent road map to do just that.

— **CYNDE MCINNIS,** founder of The Whalemobile

Andrea has helped me crush limiting beliefs, create a vision of personal fulfillment, and confidently take action to achieve personal and professional goals. Her proven system outlined in *She Thinks Big* will move you from "stuck" to "success."

— **JILL HART,** owner, Silver Pathways Consulting

It is so rare for a business book to grab your attention on the first page these days, but that is exactly what Andrea does in *She Thinks Big*. This book is a much-needed guide for all of those women who dream of starting their own businesses, moving in a new direction, or leading the next generation of business leaders. Thank you!

— **BELINDA ELLSWORTH,** author and host of the *Work from Your Happy Place* Podcast

Clarity, compassion, and courage are just some of what you gain as you read Andrea's gem of a book! As a first-time business owner, I started feeling stuck trying to move to the next level. I chose Andrea as my coach because her focus on both life AND business, and the mindset shifts that need to happen in both areas. Andrea shows that you CAN move out of that stagnant plateau you're currently on and into a flowing and growing life.

— **REBECCA D. HOGG,** owner and licensed professional, Canvas Counseling & Wellness, PLLC

She Thinks Big is a transformative gem! With wisdom, clarity, and practical guidance, Andrea offers a road map for women to embrace their dreams and step into their full potential. Through inspiring stories, thought-provoking exercises, and empowering strategies, this book encourages readers to cultivate a mindset for meaningful growth. It's a book that ignites ambition and equips women with the tools they need to create the extraordinary lives they deserve.

— **MISSY SHOPSHIRE,** author of *Forces at Work*

There is so much good to say about this book, it's hard to know where to start. *She Thinks Big* is great for any woman who is feeling stuck, for all women remembering feeling stuck and wanting to celebrate getting out of their box, and for any woman preparing to think and do big in life.

— **DIANE HELBIG,** Chief Improvement Catalyzer at Helbig Enterprises

Andrea breaks down how to untangle the daily mental knots that stop all women. She reminds us that we all have the power to think big and create our dreams at any stage of our lives. The magic happens when we shift our thinking to move past our own mess and toward our extraordinary.

— **MICHELLE CAPIZZI,** abstract artist

She Thinks Big is not only a great read, but also a great reread! Even if you believe you have a positive mindset, when life happens and chaos enters, this book is a great reminder to Think BIG, take risks, and continue to move forward with BIG DREAMS.

— **KIMBERLY GRAY MCDANIEL,** Sc.D., CEO at Intecare

In *She Thinks Big*, Andrea has outlined a new approach for the female entrepreneur to move into the extraordinary. With her step-by-step Think Big process, you are led to discover your current mindset, uncover your fears and obstacles, and move forward.

— **SARAH KHAN,** CEO/founder of Sarah Khan Yoga Retreats and Saffron and Pearls

THINK

big

TOOLKIT

*Y*ou're amazing. Go do amazing things.

My daughter has heard me say this for years. I would often whisper these words to her when she was an infant lying on her changing table. I would yell them through the window of the car in the carpool line as she walked toward the school entrance. And now I insert them into a morning text on big exam days.

This book is dedicated to you, Rebecca, and all young women.

If you Think Big, doing *amazing things* is easy.

TABLE OF CONTENTS

THE BOX IS REAL... UNTIL IT ISN'T

Knowing that things could be worse should not stop us from trying to make them better.

— **Sheryl Sandberg (Facebook)**

1 sat at my desk, trying to keep my shoulders from slumping forward. The clock on my computer informed me it was 6:00 p.m. The kids could heat up chicken nuggets again, so they were fine. Right? I had time to call Lydia before I needed to get ready for dinner plans with my husband, Rob, and our friends at 7:00.

My mind sifted through the day's events. Constantly occupied and frazzled by phone calls and emails, I had had no time to just think — and I needed to sort out what to tell Lydia. It was no big deal, I told myself. But I couldn't bring myself to dial her number.

I took a deep breath. Lydia, a 1099 contractor on paper, but an entrepreneur as far as I was concerned, was working hard to grow her business selling clothing she received each season from our parent company. I had recruited and hired Lydia through my 1099 role with this company. Now I needed to train (i.e., coach) her to be the success she (and I) knew she could be. I wished I could call and congratulate her, saying, "Guess what? They think your idea is awesome! Go ahead and bring this season's line into the law firm. Those female attorneys will love it — and you!"

But I couldn't.

Instead, I had to tell her the truth: "Lydia, I'm sorry, but the company is so rigid with rules and regulations that they just can't allow you to do anything outside those parameters."

My success depended on my ability to support and motivate my trainees — yet I constantly had to deliver these deflating messages. I knew firsthand how receiving them felt for two reasons. First, I had been Lydia just a few years ago. And second, in my current role, I had suggested plenty of my own ideas, and my boss always sounded so excited — until she came back to tell me corporate didn't want to act on them.

Glancing up from another email, I noticed it was now 6:15. I couldn't put it off any longer. I had to get ready for dinner. Sighing, I picked up the phone.

As I told Lydia the news, I realized in dismay that my voice had adopted the same tone of rueful apology as my boss's. "Hey, I'm sorry, but corporate feels your idea won't work. It's a great idea, but it's just too risky. Well, there are these factors..." I rattled off their concerns — ones I didn't even believe myself.

I could hear the brightness drain from her voice as she mentally navigated the latest wall between her and success. I was thinking what she was thinking. *Why were they trying to make this so hard?*

As I hung up, I reminded myself again why I liked my work. The work-from-home situation was perfect. I was my own boss. I could set my own hours. As an entrepreneur, I could do what I loved — coaching other entrepreneurs to succeed. The work suited my needs perfectly — corporate had even raised me from an independent seller (contractor) to a director of recruiting. They obviously recognized my potential.

Or did they? They were risk-averse and seemed to value security more than creativity or innovation. It was a "follow the rules and keep your head down" situation.

I pushed my chair back. I didn't have time to think about it. I rushed upstairs to find an outfit for the dinner I felt too tired to go to, but we'd put Sally and Stan off for weeks.

Rob arrived home as I was rushing around downstairs. He saw my face and said, "What's wrong?"

"Nothing. It's been a long day. And I can't find my purse." I continued to look around the house while he changed. As he came downstairs, I finally found my purse on the floor, half under my desk where I'd dropped it earlier.

In the car, he tried to make jokes but gave up after five minutes. We rode to the restaurant in silence, music playing low as he navigated traffic.

I hated these dinners, not because I didn't like our friends, but because I felt out of place with nothing to talk about. I was way more than "just a mom," but I didn't know how to talk about my job. Why was I always so busy? It wasn't even like the job paid a great salary. In fact, my colleagues and I used to joke that we were volunteers. Embarrassed, I would just deflect questions and fade into the woodwork, listening to the conversation.

As we drove home, Rob said, "OK, what's up with you? What happened today? You're so quiet and unhappy."

"I don't want to talk about it."

"I'm concerned. It seems you're never in a good mood lately. You barely said a word at dinner."

"I'm sorry. I just have a lot on my mind," I replied.

Back at my desk that night, I was wrapping up one last email when the realization hit me.

I was stuck. I was trying to make things work, but they weren't working. I wasn't *desperately* unhappy — I was *sort of* unhappy all around. Something didn't feel right, but I couldn't identify it. And it was taking its toll in subtle ways I didn't understand.

I kept myself busy, so much so that I had trouble keeping my head above water. I found myself snapping at the kids for no real reason. This wasn't the first time I couldn't answer when Rob asked me what was wrong.

I wasn't taking care of myself. I wasn't eating right, and I wasn't making sure the kids did, either.

Something definitely wasn't right. And the thing that wasn't right was me.

I had started working with a coach myself to level up my success. As we worked together, I uncovered even more of my issues.

I had trouble planning beyond the season — fall, winter, spring, summer — because that was how the clothing company planned. I couldn't plan a summer vacation in winter; that was too far away! And when summer rolled around, we

SOMETHING
DEFINITELY
WASN'T
RIGHT.
AND THE
THING THAT
WASN'T RIGHT
WAS *ME.*

never went anywhere except to visit family because it was too late.

When I went out with Rob, I often felt like his shadow, as if I was somehow lesser than he. He's an oncologist, and when we're out together, people often stop to thank him for helping save their lives. I would remain in the background, happy for him but wishing I could have a similar experience.

My coach suggested I leave my current position and become a coach. I scoffed at the idea. In my already exhausted brain, the thought of starting another business sounded even more exhausting. I wanted to succeed and be happy at what I was already doing. It was safe, and it checked all the important boxes, I thought.

I kept telling myself I had success, but I didn't *feel* like I had it. I was ready to have a woman in her 40s stop me in Target to tell me what an amazing impact I'd had on her life, just as people did with Rob.

Eventually, my coach and I unraveled the mental knots.

Over the last 10 years, I had trained (and coached) a large number of entrepreneurial women. To start their own businesses, they had to have belief in themselves that would fuel their success. Many of them hadn't begun with that mindset, but I helped them get there.

But while I had coached all these other women, I wasn't taking my own advice. My mindset wasn't serving me at all.

Nothing I was doing made sense. I loved helping other women succeed, but how could I do that working for a company that stifled all creativity, didn't support success, and constantly moved the goalposts? They would set a goal that meant "success," but when my colleagues and I met it, instead of celebrating, they just moved it to something harder.

We never felt like we had achieved anything. We were on a hamster wheel.

I was in a box someone else had designed, and it was too small. So why was I trying to stay there? And how could I get out?

I felt like someone had brainwashed me into thinking there was nothing better out there. Leaving my box sounded scary. Lots of unknowns lurked outside its walls. But I also never wanted to make another phone call like the one I'd made to Lydia again, and I never wanted my voice to take on that sad, apologetic tone as I delivered someone else's "no" again.

If I didn't leave, I would become just another corporate bureaucrat carrying the next "no" message, resigned to my fate.

Fear had me thinking small. To get out of this box, I needed to stretch my imagination beyond its confines, beyond what I knew, and allow what I didn't know to come in and change things. I thought of myself as daring, brave, adventurous. I needed to act like it.

I decided to be who I really was and Think Big.

It took time to come to this decision, but when I did, amazing things unfolded.

I decided to give coaching on my own a chance. I started with a trial period, working in someone else's practice as I became certified. I gave myself 12 weeks to decide. It took eight.

I realized not only did I want to be a coach; I LOVED coaching. I was all in. And I didn't want to coach in someone else's practice; I wanted to start my own coaching business. I knew if I started a coaching business on my own, I could, and would, do it on my own terms — not for me, but for the people who I could help level up.

I allowed myself to picture my success beyond what the confines of my previous thinking had allowed.

I was ready to make an income that could rival my husband's.

I was ready to emerge from the background and create a life that allowed me to live up to my potential. So I did exactly that — I stopped working for someone else and started my own business. I decided to bet on myself and open a 12-month zero-interest credit card to cover all my new business expenses, which were considerable. Paying it off before I paid any interest would indicate my success.

Before the sixth month, I received my credit card statement... and it was at a zero balance. I had met my challenge; I wouldn't pay interest.

Five years in, as I walked through Saks, a woman stopped me. "I know someone who worked with you. She raves about you. You helped her so much. She is a new person and so successful. I really need to work with you, too."

A client even stopped me at the airport as I was heading out west to ski. "I can't believe I finally get to meet you in person after all these years of coaching me via Zoom," she said. "I feel like I'm meeting my own personal celebrity. And... I thought you were a lot taller!" We both laughed.

Taller, no. But a bigger thinker who isn't afraid to go after her dreams, YES.

I want that for all my clients — and for you.

Because I realize how women get stuck and why they can't figure out how to get out. I've been there myself. If you feel frustrated, confused, stymied about how to create the freedom and the life you want, you're not alone.

And the secret isn't in some magical action you can take. It just takes a different type of work. But it's work worth doing. It's the work of getting out of your own way by changing your thinking... by changing YOU.

First, you must realize that the box isn't something someone else is giving you — it isn't external. The box is what you're giving you. The box is your own mind. If you don't know how to get it to work for you, it will work against you. And you won't know why.

And it doesn't matter who your boss is. When you're your own boss — the situation most of my clients are in — it's no different. You're still at the mercy of your mind — unless you choose not to be.

You can expand your thinking beyond its current limiting confines. This book will show you exactly why you're in the box, how to get out, and what will happen when you do. Some things may surprise you, and some may not. It's not always just knowing what to do or thinking positively — it's eavesdropping on yourself, learning what's working and what's not working for you, and knowing how to apply that knowledge and when. It's discovering who you want to become and knowing how to put it all together into a system that works.

If you're struggling to get out of your box, read on — and have hope. You can do this! It boils down to one thing:

To think beyond the box, you need to Think Big.

PART ONE

MINDSET

Clear the Clutter

CHAPTER 1

BIG PROBLEMS: AM I DOING THIS RIGHT?

The middle is messy, but it's also where all the magic happens, all the tension that creates goodness and learning.

— Brené Brown

A TALE OF TWO CLIENTS

When Lindsey came to me, chaos had engulfed her life. It should have been great. Her furniture boutique was booming — she was making over six figures. Customers were pouring in. She had hired help with marketing, sales, and working in her small warehouse, so she wasn't totally on her own.

However, she still wore a lot of hats. Inside her business, she took the roles of administrative assistant, bookkeeper, marketing director, inventory manager, purchasing coordinator, and display designer. Her business also was doing model home furnishing for some local home builders, which Lindsey handled herself. And when she got home, she had to put on her mom hat and be the taxi, disciplinarian, cook, nurse, homework helper — the list went on and on. Her husband traveled three to four nights a week, and though they had some childcare help, she had to manage that, too.

"I have to be in all places at all times and all things to all people," she told me. Her insane schedule left her with very little sleep, a frazzled mind, and the nagging feeling that maybe she had taken a wrong turn somewhere. Success had come, but it wasn't what she thought it would be.

She had always dreamed of being able to manage her own schedule, pick up her kids from school, and take a walk in the middle of the day in her beautiful neighborhood. The picture had looked so perfect when it was just a picture. It was one of the reasons she had left her corporate job — to create this ideal life she saw in her imagination. But when she hit reality, the parts she'd made come true didn't feel as she expected, and most days were too demanding to allow for 10 minutes' thought, let alone a mid-day walk away from the calls, orders, and duties she thought she should perform (whether she really *had* to is for my next book!).

As she saw it, she had three equally unappealing options. "Do I put on my big-girl pants and learn how to keep doing it all?" she asked. "Or do I throw in the towel and be a stay-at-home mom? Or maybe I should choose option three and go back to being a corporate employee."

Spinning around and around with these thoughts, she couldn't ever land anywhere — so she just kept doing what she was already doing. The minutiae of her day engulfed her in small thinking as she just tried to stay on top of it.

Around that same time, another client called me — a property manager named Carrie, who lived in Iowa.

Carrie's situation was almost the exact opposite of Lindsey's. Carrie had a comfortable, happy situation, but she wanted to transition into a new business venture that was more flexible and didn't require her to be always in Iowa. She had two main reasons for this: First, her husband would retire soon, and she anticipated wanting to spend more time with him at their second home in the Florida Keys. And second, she had a business idea she was excited about.

An expert in retirement lifestyle planning, she'd even published a book on the subject. She wanted to leverage this expertise and create a business specifically to serve a niche audience of people around five years away from retirement, helping them transition from one stage of life to the next.

Carrie knew exactly how much money she was making and exactly how much money she wanted to make moving forward. She wanted someone to help her put her ideas together and push her out of her comfort zone to create her business. She needed fresh thinking.

Most importantly, like Lindsey, she needed to Think Bigger.

THE CHALLENGE OF FINDING FULFILLMENT

On the surface, these two situations seem very different. But some common threads with both women struck me — and they're common threads for most of the clients I work with.

Both Lindsey and Carrie had mindset issues. They weren't sure how to proceed. They were afraid to make mistakes.

And they didn't just want to "find" fulfillment — as if it was the Holy Grail. They wanted to *create it for themselves* by doing what they knew they were capable of, by making things better, easier, and maybe even fun.

And both questioned whether what seemed somewhat impossible could be possible. Lindsey wondered whether she could ever get out of the chaos, believing maybe it was just associated with "this season of life." Carrie wondered if the next version of herself — Future Carrie — could even make things better than they were now because, honestly, there really wasn't anything inherently *wrong* with the current Carrie and her business. Making the shift was risky for her. She also questioned whether it was necessary. After all, one of her reasons was more time in Florida, which sounded a little luxurious to her. Did she really deserve that?

But both women knew they wanted more. They both knew if they had that elusive "more," things would be better.

YOU CAN'T ROLL ON A LOPSIDED WHEEL

At the beginning of a new coaching relationship, I take the client through an exercise where we examine all the facets of their lives (we'll talk more about this in Chapter 6). These facets include their health and wellness, financial situation, professional side, relationships, and ability to manage their time and stay organized. I ask them to rate their level of satisfaction in each of these areas on a scale from 1 to 10, with 10 being amazing and 1 being horrible. Inevitably, I get a range of numbers, with some better than others — a couple of 5s, a couple of 9s, a 7.5, a 1, etc.

Then, I ask them to imagine each of these areas as spokes on a wheel, and the numbers are the spokes' lengths in inches.

If the spokes on the wheel are all different lengths, the wheel isn't going to roll well. It will just bump along. It doesn't create movement; it hampers movement and takes up a lot more energy just to keep moving forward. Plus, it's a bumpy ride. No wonder they're feeling knocked around.

After 15 years of working with all kinds of women in a variety of roles (including myself), what I've found is that we all put a lot of effort and time into keeping the wheel rolling. And newsflash: To roll, all the spokes don't have to be 10 inches. That's not what we're after. What we're after is a smoother ride — spokes closer to the same length and longer — because a larger wheel can travel more smoothly over rough ground. We want the wheel to not only use less energy but also create more energy and flow well — maybe even coast downhill.

So, what's the problem? Well, believe it or not, half the problem is the thing we wanted and achieved in the first place — success.

THE HIDDEN TRAP: WHAT PARKING LOT ARE YOU STUCK IN?

Over the years, I've noticed some common situations when clients describe their feeling of being "stuck." They feel they want or need to be "going somewhere," but they aren't. The root problem is something you wouldn't think of as a problem: Success.

Yes, success can be a hidden trap. Current success coupled with a desire for more or for a different kind of success can create mindset issues. What's worse, if you don't have the right mindset and you fall into this trap, you may not even realize it.

My clients come to me because they've stopped moving or growing, and they don't know why. They've gotten stuck in what I like to think of as Mindset Parking Lots. Maybe you'll recognize yours in the following examples.

Parking Lot #1: Resigned Pain

You're parked in a bunch of negative emotions — guilt, resentment, emotional pain, overwhelm, etc. You're used to being here, used to feeling guilt that you don't spend enough time with your kids. You're used to feeling overwhelmed and can't imagine what it would feel like if you had your act together. You're used to operating at full throttle all the time. You're used to resenting the fact that you don't have the resources you need, and you're accustomed to the pain of not having the courage to ask for them. You've resigned yourself to the fact that "this is just how it is." But deep down, you so want to move away from all of this. Unfortunately, your internal GPS just doesn't know where to go next or how to get out. You don't even know what your destination looks like. And so you stay in the Parking Lot, suffering and wishing you could be somewhere else.

Parking Lot #2: Guilty Curiosity

Sitting in this Parking Lot is different. You feel you want to move toward something inside you — a desire. You feel a nudge. You're curious about what else is out there. You wonder if you're capable of creating or doing something more. But you're questioning that desire because there's nothing really wrong with what's going on right now. You're not in any pain; you don't feel guilt. Things are just fine the way they are. So you think about that thing you could do, but you don't tell anyone. You don't want to appear ungrateful or needy. And are you really capable of handling whatever else might come your way? You've thought about typing new destinations into your internal GPS, but you're not quite sure. So you don't go anywhere. You keep telling yourself how great your current location is and how you'd be crazy to leave.

But you can't get rid of that nudge, and it just keeps bugging you.

Parking Lot #3: Frustrated Future

In this Parking Lot, you know what you want, and you have been trying to get there, but nothing seems to work. It's frustrating because you know your stuff. Getting to where you currently are required building a lot of systems and processes from scratch. You learned a lot getting here, and all the systems and processes you've created are working great — and yet, they aren't taking you to the next place you want to go. Maybe you want to expand your business, add a new dimension, or even move to a different phase of your life. After trying and not getting results using what you have, you've become frustrated and exasperated. You feel like a failure even though you're successful. Often, you think you just want to quit the whole thing because it's no longer serving you. It feels like a liability — an obstacle keeping you from going where you want to go now.

You don't want to expend any more effort or brain power. You're burned out. You're done.

LINDSEY'S AND CARRIE'S PARKING LOTS

Lindsey was definitely in Parking Lot #1 and hovering in #2 with some guilt. She was afraid to admit to most people in her inner circle what she really wanted. She talked about it with her husband, but he wasn't in her business. He didn't experience what she was experiencing with customers and managing her hired help. And he certainly wasn't feeling or seeing what she was seeing at home because he wasn't there that much.

She had started asking herself what she wanted, but even those questions were hard to focus on. A friend asked her how her business was going, and she said, "It's just going." Not the answer she wanted to give, such as, "It's great," or, "It's thriving," or, "I'm loving it."

Carrie, on the other hand, fell into Parking Lot #3. She had already asked herself what she wanted and wasn't afraid to admit it. But she had tried to get there using what she knew, and that just wasn't working. She felt like she was spinning her wheels.

Things get even more complicated when you're straddling more than one of the above parking lots — or meandering around from one to the other. Knowing there's a problem, yet being unable to pinpoint it, can not only zap all your energy, but it can also make you feel hopeless.

WHEN TO ASK FOR HELP

When you're spinning from one option to another and never making a decision, something has to give. It's time to ask for help. You know it when you get there. Sometimes, it takes a trigger.

When Lindsey heard herself giving her half-hearted answers about her business, she finally admitted her methods weren't working. She decided to reach out to me to help her clarify what she really wanted and determine whether it was possible. She realized she just wasn't figuring it out on her own.

Carrie felt stuck and alone. When she heard me on a podcast talking about the importance of having a guide or Sherpa along the journey with you as you climb the mountain to reach your goal, she realized she wanted that partner. She needed someone to be a co-pilot to help work out her ideas and make sense of them. She might be able to do it alone, but she might not, and it was taking way too long to figure that out.

WHEN YOU'RE
SPINNING
FROM ONE
OPTION TO
ANOTHER AND
NEVER MAKING
A DECISION,
SOMETHING
HAS TO GIVE.
IT'S TIME TO
ASK FOR HELP.

THE REAL PROBLEM

Here's the truth: What keeps you stuck in the Parking Lot is fear.

In every one of the three Parking Lots, the trap isn't success — it's the fear of driving out of the lot toward the success you crave. When you're successful, you have something to lose. You have new risks you didn't have before. The greater your success, the longer you may be stuck in the trap if you're not in the right mindset.

Fear shows up as confusion, indecision, and self-judgment. It makes you start redefining success over and over. It keeps you thinking small. Small thoughts aren't risky. Small actions are safe. Doing the same old thing is comfortable, even when you're steeped in chaos or unhappiness at not reaching your potential. Trying to reach your potential is scary when you have something to lose. Besides, if you're successful, haven't you already reached your potential?

Wrangling the fear is a risk, too. When you're too afraid of the answers, you won't ask yourself the tough questions.

But the right questions and answers are required to reveal the cause of the faulty engine — the underlying fears — and then, ultimately, to forge full speed ahead.

NINE COMMON FEARS OF SUCCESSFUL ENTREPRENEURIAL WOMEN

What are the scariest things for a successful entrepreneurial woman? I find they all fall into three major categories: Fear of the unknown, fear of failing, and fear of lack of resources.

Fear of the Unknown

When you fear the unknown, what you really fear is your capability to react to new events. You don't have confidence in yourself to handle things no matter what. This shows up in four main ways.

1. **Fear of uncertainty:** When you run a business, you want things nailed down. You don't like it when you can't control what could happen. You start to fear what you don't know. What you don't know becomes a strange, blank space. When you focus on it, it grows. It takes over, and suddenly, you feel like you don't know anything at all. Since you don't know, you don't plan. With no plan, you don't act. What action should you take? You don't know.

   You project all the horrible things that could happen into that blank space. Of course, you don't want to move forward. Just look at all those potential catastrophes waiting there. Faced with the Blank Spot of Impending Catastrophe, you just shut down.

2. **Fear of change:** This is like fear of uncertainty, but it usually focuses on fear of a specific outcome of an action you might take or something new that enters your world. In this, you've identified the threat as change. Change creates another opening for new problems to enter your world. New problems create uncertainty — and we're back to that Blank Spot of Impending Catastrophe again. Decision made! We now most certainly do not want to take that action we were considering.

3. **Fear of risk:** As an entrepreneur, you already carry the responsibility of running an entire business. You have no protective corporate network to shield you from your failures. Your decisions seem to carry a greater weight of risk because the whole business could be at stake. You want to think more before you make decisions. This can be a great strategy, but when you fear taking ANY risk and seek only the security of what you've always done, you'll eventually cripple your success.

I even see this with clients on consult calls who really want to engage in coaching but just can't pull the trigger. "What if this doesn't work?" they worry. So they decide to "think about it." When I ask what they are thinking about, they reply, "I don't know." They are really just delaying risk.

4. **Fear of success:** Success sounds good, but underneath its rewarding factors, it also brings change. Change means venturing into the unknown, where we can't predict things — and here we are, staring at the Blank Spot of Impending Catastrophe again.

Fear of Failure

Fear of failure is another kind of confidence issue, but it revolves around judgment — or feelings. Bad feelings. According to *Global Entrepreneurship Monitor*, of the individuals surveyed globally who believe there are good business opportunities in their local area, 19 to 60 percent (depending on the country) would still not start a business due to their fear of failure.[1] It's not a baseless assumption that the same type of fear may also hamper current entrepreneurs who want to try new things. If you judge the environment as risky or your skills as "not good enough," these judgments will lead you to fear failing.

5. **Fear of not being good enough:** This is self-judgment. When you look at yourself and constantly find your-self wanting new skills or knowledge, you'll cripple your success.

6. **Fear of being *seen* as not good enough:** Fear of failure is linked in the minds of many women to self-worth and pride. Thinking about what other people will think about your possible failure creates a picture of humiliation.

7. **Fear of letting others down:** The unwritten rule that women need to be there for their families and to manage their homes still exists. Its validity is beside the point; the assumption causes many to question whether success is even possible for wom-en. Do you have to sacrifice your responsibilities to your family to achieve it? Being seen as someone who neglects her family doesn't sound appealing. And then there's the fear of letting down people we have made commitments to — extended family, clients, friends, neighbors, volunteer organizations we signed up for, or even your team. When we don't follow through, people will be disappointed. Will they judge us as unreliable? Then, we may try to juggle even *more* commitments to show others we care and want to help.

Fear of Lack

The last fear revolves around not having enough of something
— mainly money and time, two of our biggest resources.

8. **Fear of not enough money:** Money gives you power
    to do things, especially in your business. What if you
    don't have enough? What if you don't make enough to
    support your family's needs? What if you don't have
    enough to cover emergencies? (It's my hope that in
    the second edition of this book, I'll add "Fear of mak-
    ing too much money" to this list.)

9. **Fear of not enough time:** Sometimes, the fear of not
    having enough time to get everything done can para-
    lyze you. If you keep measuring the time you don't
    have, you won't be able to choose your priorities.
    Everything will seem huge. What if you're doing the
    wrong thing with what little time you have?

IT'S TIME TO THINK BIG

High-achieving women are used to taking action to solve
problems. I don't know how many times I've heard something like, "Just tell me what to do. I'm good at following
directions. I just need a map." They want the One Quick Fix
that will suddenly make everything better.

Unfortunately, it's not that simple. In this situation, it's
not all about the action — or at least, not the kind of action
we first think about.

The secret is to use both mindset and action in the right combination for your situation. And here's the other challenge: It keeps changing. Just when you think you've mastered your business, the next version of the business appears.

This book doesn't give you a cookie-cutter approach to solving every business problem. It doesn't give you a wand that will magically resolve your dissatisfaction, either. What it does give you is a set of tools that will allow you to see your situation differently so it will not seem so overwhelming. You can solve your problems once you learn how to Think Big.

Here's what we'll explore:

Big Mindset: In this section, you start to address your need to dream, believe, and decide Bigger as you go through the phases of your business development, whether you're a one-woman show or a multi-million-dollar business with a team. We'll deal with your fear and look at common pitfalls so you can avoid them and stay on track.

Big Plans: Even if you think you understand goals (and maybe don't like them!), I'll give you a new way to think about them, as well as a practical guide to plan, create, and assess Bigger, and use tools and systems to do it all, understanding when it's time to repeat the cycle.

Big Results: You'll be ready with the right mindset and the emotional courage to last through the ups and downs — knowing that it is a cycle — a spiral in which you're constantly expanding and growing. You'll no longer fall into the success trap — instead, you'll learn how to enjoy a new definition of freedom in every stage of business.

JUST WHEN YOU THINK YOU'VE *MASTERED* YOUR BUSINESS, THE NEXT VERSION OF THE BUSINESS *APPEARS.*

Now that we've explored the real underlying problems and looked at where our journey will take us, are you ready to meet your fear head-on? Let's go do that in the next chapter. But first, let's reflect on this one.

> ### *Bonus Resources: Think Big Toolkit*
>
> Want more? I've created some supplemental resources to help guide you through your self-discovery and planning process, both during and beyond your time with this book. Get them at **AndreaLiebross.com/toolkit** (do it now before you forget!).

THINK BIGGER: WHAT ABOUT YOU?

When I first worked with a coach, she told me to read a book with reflection exercises. I was diligent about actually following through on completing the exercises, and I am 100 percent sure doing the reflections made a huge difference in my path moving forward. It became so much easier to "see" what was happening in my brain and get the clarity I craved. So to get the most out of this book, I strongly advise you to do these Think Bigger reflections and the other exercises provided.

It's also good to keep a journal and track your thoughts and ideas so you can reflect on them, especially if you aren't working directly with a coach.

People often need conversation to extract the thoughts and ideas they can't get to by themselves. Journaling is the next best thing because a journal is a conversation with yourself.

TO GET *THE MOST* OUT OF THIS BOOK, I STRONGLY ADVISE YOU TO DO THESE *THINK BIGGER REFLECTIONS* AND THE OTHER EXERCISES PROVIDED.

You can find a free download that guides you through the reflections for each chapter in the Think Big Toolkit available on my website. Use the downloads or a blank notebook to answer the questions below.

For this chapter, I'd like you to think about some of the information and apply it to yourself.

1. How did you feel as you read Lindsey's story? What elements can you relate to?

2. What about Carrie's story? Was there anything in her experience you could relate to?

3. Now, think about yourself. If I were telling your story in this book, what would I say? What would your main issues or needs be?

4. So, why did you pick up this book?

5. What do you hope to solve by reading this book? If you answer, "I don't know," that's fine. That's where a lot of my clients start out. Just tell the truth about your situation. Acknowledging the places where you say, "I do know," is a start.

CHAPTER 2

BIG COURAGE: FACE YOUR FEAR

It takes a lot of courage to show your dreams to someone else.

— Erma Bombeck

rittany and her husband run an IT business handling onsite commercial installations and providing ongoing technical support. When she came to me, she had identified a LOT of problems she was ready to deal with: She was the only one in her business who could sell their products because clients only wanted to talk to her. She was the lead installer, which she handled in addition to sales, while her husband handled design and tech support. She had challenges with getting clients to pay a big deposit — "No one wants to do it," she said.

In her personal life, she didn't feel great about the job she was doing as a mom. "I just don't like doing 'mom things,'" she said.

"What are 'mom things'?" I asked.

"You know, like decorating bedroom doors on birthdays or bringing cupcakes to class," she explained, adding that her daughter's 13th birthday certainly wasn't going to be featured on Pinterest.

Personally, she had some goals, too. She wanted to exercise more but couldn't fit it into her schedule. The five hours sleep per night wasn't cutting it — she was tired all the time. Even meal planning was a chore. "If I have to think about what's for dinner one more time, I'm going to lose it!" she said.

She was convinced she had a time management problem. There weren't enough hours in the day (yet) for her to be an amazing business owner, a good mom, and kind to herself.

Having identified the problem, she now felt a glimmer of hope. She could figure it out. She was a creative, after all. She was great at solving problems.

However, none of her solutions worked.

Her brain was always in a hundred different places. Unable to turn the dial to focus and stay there, it constantly barraged her with ideas and thoughts. In a classic example of shiny object syndrome, it darted from "I needed to fill out this form for Bobby's surf camp" to "When am I gonna fit in a trip to the grocery store?" to "I need to work on that design for the prospective client" to "we need to do invoicing" — all within the span of sixty seconds. The constant onslaught exhausted her.

"Andrea, just tell me what to do," she said. "I'm great at adhering to instructions. If you give me the steps to figuring out how to get what I want, then we'll be good. I don't let people down. I follow directions."

Getting what she wanted was a theme. When I asked her how she found me, she'd replied, "I Googled, 'How do I get what I want?' and your name came up."

Yet over the next few weeks, the things we worked on still didn't address the issue. She had trouble choosing which action to take, so she didn't take any. She seemed to be spinning, and we couldn't figure out why.

After some digging, I suspected the real issue was that she *really didn't know what she wanted*. What she *thought* she wanted wasn't what she *actually wanted*. Even clarifying what she didn't want was a challenge.

We were a month or two into our sessions when things suddenly became clear.

In an offhand conversation, Brittany revealed she was starting another business. She had an idea and had already lined up investors. And the process was in motion for it to launch. But only she could take the next steps, and the elements for those had been sitting on her desk for weeks. She "just needed to focus on them." But she didn't have time because her current business and personal life demanded all her attention.

"I want to be at a place where my current business runs like clockwork," she said. "Where I have the right people. Where I have systems. Where clients are coming in without much effort. If our established business could run on its own, and I could focus my time and energy on this new start-up, life would be amazing," she said.

Aha!

This was the real reason she wasn't taking action. All the action we had planned was on the things she *didn't want* to do but thought she *should* be doing. She had been telling herself she needed to manage her time efficiently to get in "all the things" — but that wasn't really what she wanted to do at all.

What she REALLY wanted was to run that second business (which would make her millions) while just being an overseer or the visionary of the first. Why hadn't she realized that?

This kind of situation shows why having a coach is so helpful. With this breakthrough, I decided to press her further.

"What else do you want?" I asked. "If I could sprinkle magic fairy dust over all of Southern California, what would appear?"

"Well, there's a piece of property I've had my eye on for years. It's in the foothills. It's beautiful. I've even attempted to buy it. But things haven't worked out... yet. What I want is to buy it and design and build a house for my family to live in. And have another structure on the property that would serve as our business headquarters. We would have land and everything all together on one piece of property."

"What else do you want?"

"I want my kids to be happy. I want them to remember me as a fun mom who loves them. I want to spend time with them. We love to travel. Fact: We traveled around the US in a camper for a year. That was some of the best time I've ever spent with them. I want to be a present parent."

"What else do you want?"

"I want to be 30 pounds lighter. I want to exercise every day. I want someone to do my grocery shopping and only select things that will fuel my body. I want a personal chef. I'm tired of making dinner."

"What else?"

This one really hit me. "I want to leave a legacy. I don't want to die before I achieve any of the things I mentioned before. And my fear is that I'll run out of time. Life is too short to get everything you want. But something is holding me back from trying — with all-out effort — to go for it. To go after my dreams."

There it was.

What was holding her back — what had been keeping her from even accepting what she really wanted — was her belief that none of this was possible, and she feared she was running out of time. So she wasn't working at full force to create any of these things she wanted.

Fear was undermining everything she was trying to do.

Her fear that she would be remembered as not such a great mom was undermining her efforts to be a great mom.

Her fear that her existing business couldn't run without her was holding her back from hiring help, shifting responsibilities, and creating better systems so her husband could run it without her.

Her fear that her start-up business idea would be a flop — that there would be no clicks to buy her product and that investors wouldn't keep investing — was holding her back on taking the next steps.

Her fear about what would happen to the first business if this second business was a success was also holding her back.

And all these fears affected everything else, too. By not working to further either of these businesses, she wasn't generating enough revenue to support her dream of buying property and building her own home and office, which was just disappointing.

Her fear that putting time toward exercise and herself would take away time from money-making opportunities prevented her from feeling good about herself physically.

Fear was eating up Brittany's life — and it had her thinking small, playing small, and staying small.

It had to stop.

"Pretend you're in a helicopter circling Southern California, and you're looking down on yourself. What do you see?" I asked.

"I see a frantic, exhausted woman guzzling Starbucks, living a chaotic life," she said.

Brittany saw what I saw — this woman was scared. And her fears were undermining her efforts — but the woman herself didn't see that because she had some dark sunglasses on.

I felt for her, especially because it didn't have to be that way. What I needed to do was convince her of that.

What she wanted was possible. All it would take was switching out her sunglasses... and believing in herself.

We had more work to do — but it was the real work we needed to do, and it was definitely worth doing.

What Brittany really needed was to learn to Think Big.

WHAT FEAR LOOKS LIKE

I have a saying: Being an entrepreneur is a journey in personal development disguised as an entrepreneurial adventure. When we're on an adventure, it's normal to feel some fear — otherwise, it wouldn't be an adventure. Part of the adventure is learning to face and overcome fear to accomplish what we've set out to achieve.

BEING AN ENTREPRENEUR IS A JOURNEY IN *PERSONAL DEVELOPMENT* DISGUISED AS AN ENTREPRENEURIAL *ADVENTURE.*

To face your fear, you have to realize you're afraid. That seems obvious, but it's not, especially when admitting fear is also frightening. Getting inside your own head can often be like trying to read the label from inside the peanut butter jar. It feels impossible. Often, a coach or someone "outside the jar" can be indispensable for deciphering the label.

If you're not sure what you're feeling, one way to find out is to look at what you're doing. Thoughts lead to feelings, feelings lead to actions, and actions lead to results.

Let's look at some actions that indicate fear is present. In my experience, fear manifests itself in ways that fall under the umbrella of what I call "buffering." If you own an Apple computer, you're probably familiar with that Rainbow Circle of Doom that spins around and around as you wait… forever. Something is downloading that gives the computer the message, "we're not quite ready to take the action you requested," and delays that next step. And if it never does what you want it to do, you sometimes have to Force Quit out of it and start over.

Humans buffer, too. For us, it looks something like this:

Seeking more knowledge. And more. Reading the whole internet may not be enough. You believe that once you know that elusive bit of information, you can do That Important Thing. You don't really know what you're looking for, but you'll know when you find it. Maybe. It will be that One Magic Piece of Knowledge that will make everything about doing That Important Thing clear.

Wearing the Busy Badge. "Hello, My Name Is: BUSY." This badge is your shield of protection against not doing That

Important Thing. Yes, you need to do it — but you're far too busy. You're doing the kind of things you can check off to give you that little dopamine hit that tells you you're accomplished and productive. You return the quick email, schedule the appointment, pick up the kids, empty the dishwasher, cook the meal, handle the crisis. You're much too busy to add That Important Thing to your plate right now.

Waiting for Event X. Well, of course you need to do That Important Thing, and you will — just as soon as Event X happens. Event X can be anything that needs to happen or be over with, or even be recovered from. You'll do it "after I get back from vacation," "when the kids go back to school," "when my business is more established," "when I have more money." And you really mean it... but there always seems to be another Event X preventing you from completing That Important Thing.

Asking for more opinions... and more. You're not sure how many are "enough." You've assembled a crowd of thousands, but they don't seem quite adequate. You're not sure why you still can't seem to find that Golden Stamp of Approval you're waiting for, but you're sure the next person will have it. Until then, it's fun to talk about your idea and get more ideas about how your idea might work.

Planning but not executing. You've read every book on planning and time management. You have every planning tool in your arsenal — organizers, apps, computer programs, project management tools. You're a planning queen. You've got a lot of lists. And you're a master at iCal. You spend two hours each day deciding how you're going to spend your day and decorating your planner with stickers and illustrations using highlighters and colored pens. It looks gorgeous! But then everything goes out the window as the next crisis rolls in. You can't seem to make the world revolve around your planner, and nothing you plan ever seems to happen.

Spinning from one idea to the next. You know you should do That Important Thing, but That Other Important Thing seems so much more important — except you've been putting it off because That New Thing has captured your attention. That New Thing may or may not be important, but it is so interesting! If only you had more time to focus on That New Thing — and then there's That Lingering Thing. Ugh. That Lingering Thing has been sitting on your plate for three months. You don't even remember why it is there, but you're sure it was important — maybe you should go check your notes. Ah, notes! That's right; you need to buy a new notebook — better add that to the shopping list. Wait — shopping? If you're out shopping, you could pick up that little black dress for the party next Saturday. And then there are groceries...

WHEN ACTION ISN'T REALLY ACTION

All the preceding behaviors fall into a category of activity that Master Certified Life Coach Brooke Castillo, founder of the Life Coach School, refers to as "passive action."[2]

She believes there are two kinds of action: passive action and massive action.

Passive action often feels like the "Fred Flintstone running" version of action. You know the old cartoon where Fred Flintstone takes off running, except there's that pause where his feet are moving, and he's not getting anywhere? Even in his "car" (which is also foot-powered), he has this issue.

That's what passive action is. We're doing lots of things, but we're not getting anywhere.

We can overload on passive action, spending hours searching and scrolling and looking for answers, asking a hundred closest friends what they think we should do, listening to every podcast (and I love podcasts!), and busying ourselves with all the tasks that don't move the needle.

However, what we need isn't passive action but massive action. Massive action drives results.

Massive action:

- Creates things
- Makes decisions
- Makes money
- Tells the truth

Massive action requires focus, discipline, and commitment. It feels hard and uncomfortable when we're doing it but amazing and satisfying when we're done.

If you've been doing "all the things" and you still haven't moved the needles that matter, look at what you've been doing. What kind of action is it? I'll bet that most of it falls into the passive action category.

Some women even go so far as to try to label their identities with passive action labels. "I am better under pressure." Or, "I'm just a procrastinator. It's just who I am."

When in reality, no one is "just a procrastinator." Underneath, you procrastinate for a reason. You're buffering, and you already know why.

Fear is sneaking in and claiming your headspace.

It's tough to face that, I know — but massive action tells the truth, right? So let's look at the truth of what you could be afraid of and start wrangling this thing into shape.

TAKE CHARGE OF YOUR FEAR

By identifying the source of your fears, you've taken the first step toward flipping your script to a different response. To do that, let's look at the nature of fear in humans. Why does it exist in the first place? Once you know what you're dealing with, it will get much clearer.

The Motivational Triad

When we stay stuck in safety mode, even when we're in a painful situation, it's because something called the "motivational triad"[3] is hard at work. The motivational triad refers to a theory that there are three main factors related to motivation:

- Seeking pleasure
- Avoiding pain
- Conserving energy

Our brains are hardwired to seek pleasure, avoid pain, and conserve energy. We're still wired the way we were during the caveman (or cavewoman) days. We still respond to pain and pleasure in the same way, and we still naturally conserve energy.

These are survival instincts people needed when they ventured out of the cave and had to worry about getting eaten by a saber-toothed tiger or when they didn't have farming or Tupperware and refrigerators and had to rely on hunting and gathering for food. They might go a long time without eating, so they needed to conserve their body's energy for important tasks.

However, we no longer need the motivational triad in the 21st century. No one is going to eat us if we step outside of our cave. No one is there waiting to clock us over the head with a club.

Nevertheless, it takes effort to confront this type of thinking and give equal airtime to new thinking and new beliefs. How do you talk some sense into your inner cavewoman?

The only way is by using your brain to manage her instead of listening to her — and to make your fears work *for* you instead of against you.

FOUR STRATEGIES FOR HARNESSING FEAR

Your fear is coming from your inner cavewoman, so you must think beyond her to manage her. Here are four great ways to start doing that.

1. Consider Your Thought Options

How we feel is the number-one driver of how we react. When you don't acknowledge how you feel, it will still affect your responses — you just won't *know* it.

When you care about others, you ask how they're doing. You might even drop in on them or just give them a call. Why not do that with yourself? Drop in on your brain. What's going on with it?

Our thoughts control our feelings. The goal, the project, other people, the weather, they don't control how we feel. Our *thoughts* about the goal, the project, other people, and the weather control our feelings. We can learn how to change how we feel by learning how to choose our thoughts. We have *thought options*, and depending on the option we choose, we'll feel a certain way. So we can choose a thought that doesn't create fear.

For example, my client Stephanie is a professional organizer. Representing her existing clients, she carries herself with confidence. But when trying to sell herself to new clients, she tries to fade into the background. She doesn't like selling or promoting herself.

"It feels very icky," she told me.

She related herself to a diminutive, soft-spoken female character in Police Academy named Hooks. Hooks is forever apologetically trying to get people to listen to her when even she doesn't seem sure she has anything useful to say. "Excuse me, excuse me," she will say as the crowd keeps talking.

Stephanie's fear-based thoughts tell her she's bothering people, and she predicts they won't want what she has to offer. To counter that attitude, we're working on changing her thoughts to, "I have something they need! Sharing the value I bring to the table serves them. I would be remiss not to." These thoughts will bring more confidence.

Another way to control thoughts is by thinking differently about failure. What if, instead of win-or-lose situations, you defined outcomes as *winning or learning*? Suddenly, there's no such thing as failure. There's just learning.

2. Target the Real Problem

In a coaching situation, clients often start out telling me all the details of what is going on and all their history. But I am notorious for cutting them short and asking, "so what's the problem?" This is a showstopper. They often cannot answer that question.

In the end, the real problem is almost invariably the fact that they don't want to feel a negative feeling. Often, a negative feeling is the worst thing they can experience.

Good news! We can change that experience — keep reading.

3. Embrace Ambiguity

Uncertainty is a real and constant fear. Uncertainty and ambiguity are inherent in entrepreneurship. They never leave. You'll always have the unknown... and even unknowns about the unknown!

Recognizing you'll never have all the information is important. The Blank Spot of Impending Catastrophe doesn't *have* to hold Impending Catastrophe. That's your cavewoman brain that loves catastrophizing.

Instead, why not project Impending Awesomeness? Why not look forward to the unknown? Wouldn't it be boring to always know everything that is going to happen? None of the gifts you get on birthdays or holidays would be a surprise. You would know everything everyone was going to do, always.

At a retreat I just led, I didn't tell the attendees what we were doing next until we got to that point. They *loved* it. Sometimes it's so much more fun to just go with the flow and not control everything.

4. Seek Support

For entrepreneurs who constantly battle the fear of failure, mentors, coaches, and support networks can be vital sources of reassurance because they can support the other three strategies.

According to *Harvard Business Review* researchers James Hayton and Gabriella Cacciotti, beginners and seasoned entrepreneurs benefit from a community of peers who are in any stage of business growth and of life. "These communities provide formal or informal access to those with more experience," the researchers wrote. "By belonging to a community, they learn that feelings of uncertainty and worry are commonplace, as well as which issues are deserving of attention and which will fix themselves over time."[4] This is the number-one reason why a lot of the coaching I offer takes place within a coaching community.

According to Hayton and Cacciotti, "Fear of failure is widespread and has both negative and positive effects on motivation, decision-making, and behavior." Fear, while motivating, can also create more stress, leading to health ramifications and unsustainable progress. We'll examine this more in upcoming chapters. The important thing to note is that fear is normal in entrepreneurship, and business owners must accept that and know how to handle it.

That ability can only come from changing the underlying things that are creating your fear — your thoughts, especially your beliefs. We'll look at those in the next chapter. First, let's do a short exercise.

THINK BIGGER: MANAGE YOUR FEARS

To manage your fears, you first must identify them. As you can see by reading Brittany's story, sometimes that's difficult. Sometimes, the fear prevents you from even knowing it's there. Even that is scary.

However, we're going to try to uncover some of the things you're dealing with so you can turn fear into fuel. With that in mind, look back at the nine common fears and see if you can relate to any of them.

1. What am I most afraid of? (There may be more than one thing.)

2. How has my emotional state (i.e., feelings) affected my success? What areas of my life are suffering due to these feelings?

3. How is my fear affecting my behavior (i.e., actions)? What have I been avoiding? What have I been doing more of — passive action, busy work, or just finding escape activities?

4. If I could sprinkle my own magic fairy dust over my life and make everything how I want it to be, what's the biggest thing I would change right away?

CHAPTER 3

BIG BELIEF:
THE GAME-CHANGER

*Believe Big. The size of your success is
determined by the size of your belief.*

— David J. Schwartz

One of my clients, Arianna, is a freelance commercial photographer who caters to the marketing industry. After starting her small business and creating some initial processes and systems, she was making more than six figures. She wanted to find ways to make more money, but she feared sharing her desire with her husband and the world because it felt like she was asking for *too much*. She also knew that to make more money, she would have to revamp some of her processes and procedures, hire more photographers and/or photoshop experts, and raise her prices. Each of these held concern for her, so she kept hesitating to do them.

She feared having a conversation with her husband because she wasn't sure how he would react for a few different reasons. First, they didn't need more money; they were doing fine. Arianna wondered if she should even have this desire. What would he think of her? Would he judge her for not being grateful enough for what they had? Or be mad at her for trying to make his life harder?

Second, she believed putting time toward revamping processes meant she wouldn't be spending as much time as she was now with her kids. Was this really true? And if it was, she would have to relinquish childcare responsibilities to someone else. She knew her husband's brain would immediately go to the possibility that he would have to help out more with childcare. How would he perceive all of this? Was this the ultimate sign of a bad mom, someone who would rather spend their time on their business than with their kids?

Third, hiring more help meant she had to trust someone to produce work that was up to her standards. Plus, she would have to pay them. Would the investment pay off? What if their work didn't live up to the standards she desired? Her reputation was on the line.

And finally, raising her prices was a risk. Was she good enough to demand that type of pricing in her geographic market? Could she pitch to the larger agencies that were handling major corporate brands? She did feel like she was worth that investment in general — outside her market. But she feared her current clientele, who were more mid-level agencies, wouldn't support that pricing. Was she going to lose potential clients?

Arianna was at a standstill.

WHAT'S THE WORST THING THAT COULD HAPPEN?

When I work with clients on moving past their fears, my first step is always asking them the question, "What is the worst thing that could happen?" What horrible things could happen if you changed your thinking and took action or had the hard conversations?

Most of the time, the worst thing that could happen isn't worse than staying stuck in one place. The worst thing that could happen is a feeling.

Figure 3.1 The Messy Middle

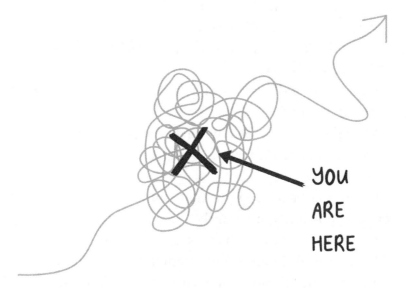

Things were going along fine... until they weren't. Welcome to the messy middle, where nothing seems quite right, and you can't figure out what's wrong. It can feel confusing, even overwhelming — and the only way to navigate your way out is to do the right work to untangle the mess.

Is experiencing a negative feeling for a short amount of time worse than feeling like you do right now? Because, after all, you don't feel so great right now, either. Even if you feel bad after taking action, wouldn't a bad feeling with action be better than a bad feeling at a standstill?

Arianna thought about what would happen if she shared what she wanted with her husband. "I guess the worst thing that could happen is that he would say, 'I think that's crazy. You should just stick with what you've got going right now. I need you. Your kids need you. Stop dreaming. Isn't what you have now good enough?'"

So I asked her, "If he did say that, how would you feel?"

"I wouldn't feel so great," she said. "He could also say he doesn't want to be with someone who has dreams to create a bigger, more profitable business than his. And if that were the case, I don't think I'd want to be with him either."

"How likely is that?"

"Well... not really very likely," she admitted. "It kind of sounds ridiculous."

"All right — so maybe having a conversation isn't so bad. What would happen if you put some additional time toward your processes?"

"I wouldn't be able to put that time toward other things — most importantly, my family."

"So, who would be with the kids?" I asked.

"My husband. Their grandparents. A babysitter."

"A dad spending more time with his kids. Does that sound so horrible? Grandparents who adore their grandchildren having an opportunity to care for them. How does that sound? And even a babysitter would bring some new ideas and different ways to play into their world. How does that sound?"

Arianna was now smiling a little. "That actually all sounds just fine. And my fear of what they would think that meant about me, leaving them with someone else, is really absurd."

Next, we tackled hiring additional help.

"The worst thing that could happen is that the new person wouldn't do a good job," Arianna said.

"And what would you do then?"

"I'd let them go," she said.

"How long would it take to recognize whether or not this person actually produced good work?"

"Oh, I can figure that out within the first day or so."

"So you wouldn't have spent too much money or time on them yet?"

"No, no," She replied. "And I can find another option very quickly. There are tons of photographers."

The worst thing that could happen in this case was a period of trial and error with a few new editors. But in the long run, the potential for taking work off her plate clearly was a big win over having to do all the work herself.

Now we tackled the worst-case pricing scenario.

"I guess the worst thing would be if people won't pay the prices, and I won't have the work."

"OK. But we just discussed how you want to work less. Would having fewer clients paying higher prices be worse than having more clients paying lower prices? Suppose you had 10 clients paying $10,000. Is that worse than 20 clients paying $5,000 each?"

The irony of her fear hit her. "No! The lower client number is better! Serving 20 clients would take much more time than 10," she replied.

MEET YOUR FRENEMY

Now is a good time to bring up someone I call your *Frenemy.*

She looks like a friend. She wants to protect you. But listening to her will keep you stuck in your Parking Lot. She's the one who lives in the back of your mind and constantly brings up scary things to remind you how vulnerable and potentially in danger you are. But what she says is just based on fear, not facts.

In Arianna's case, a lot of assumptions lurked in the back of her mind, whispering, though she didn't quite realize it. To address them, we had to bring them out into the light and make them state their case. Then it was a whole different situation.

Just like Arianna's, my Frenemy regularly reminds me of how dangerous or uncomfortable something might become. You have one, too. We all do, powered by our motivational triad.

"Do NOT have that conversation," my Frenemy says. "Do NOT do that hard thing." And then she collects all sorts of evidence that supports all the reasons why not. And they might sound good, but only if I'm in cavewoman mode.

Instead, I respond, "Today, THE REAL ANDREA is going to stand up and have the conversation and do the hard things because Andrea is someone who thinks BIG and knows that thinking BIG and doing hard things is the only way to create success."

The Frenemy acts like your friend, but she doesn't believe in you. She wants to keep you safe because that's her job, and in doing it, she often prevents you from moving forward with your best ideas. Do you really want to listen to her? Is she really your friend?

The Frenemy is wired to give you these worst-case scenarios. The more you listen to her, the less you're considering the best-case scenarios — the ones that are a HELL YES! These are the ones that make you come alive. Shouldn't they get airtime?

It's time we Think Bigger than the Frenemy does.

LEAVE YOUR LIMITING BELIEFS

When your Frenemy is talking, you start believing her. Your thoughts about yourself start to look like hers.

"I can't..." "I'm not..." "It won't..." "I don't..."

These limiting beliefs hold you back more frequently and more deeply than any external factor.

What do I mean by a *limiting belief*? I'm talking about an assumption about the wider world, about other people, or maybe, hardest of all, about ourselves.

It goes like this. You think about doing something, and then you think about why you can't or shouldn't. "I want to pitch my idea to the client, but he will think I'm too pushy." "I want to try changing up my team roles, but it probably won't work out because people will get upset." Sometimes, obviously, you shouldn't take action. If you're thinking about doing something illegal or unethical, your limiting belief will keep you out of trouble.

But most of the trouble limiting beliefs keep you out of is trouble you want — success, new challenges, achievements.

According to performance coach Michael Hyatt, "A limiting belief is a misunderstanding of the present that short-changes our future."[5]

Limiting beliefs aren't facts. They are also not just thoughts. A belief, by its very definition, is the acceptance that a statement is true. That acceptance part is critical. You're accepting statements as true when you really have no idea if they're true for YOU. In order for something to be true, you would have to be able to prove it in a court of law. Consider that when you accept a truth.

Now for the *limiting* part. A limiting belief is any statement that argues for your limits. You make a case about why you aren't what you wish you were, why the world isn't what you want it to be, why you shouldn't do that thing you want to do... or why you shouldn't even want it in the first place.

Many of Arianna's assumptions and anticipations about her situation came from limiting beliefs. She anticipated her husband would be upset because she assumed he wants her available 24/7, taking full responsibility for the household and kids and not running her own business. She assumed devoting time toward process development would create an unmanageable homelife. She thought her clients would balk at paying her prices. None of those things were true; they were just possibilities she hadn't confirmed — yet they were operating as truths.

Sometimes a limiting belief isn't about what someone isn't (or what you aren't), but it's about what you are. Remember those labels? "I'm just a procrastinator." "I'm just bad at math." "I'm just absent-minded." "I'm just always late." All of those are limiting beliefs. They excuse your limits, your inaction, and your potential future failures. They give you an escape clause so you don't have to feel bad.

You can even use them to limit your expectations of others and predict their failure in advance. "He's not very organized, so he probably won't get that done." "That older candidate is probably set in his ways; I don't want to hire him." "Meg never completes anything on time, so I can't give this assignment to her."

Limiting beliefs come from anywhere — things Past You experienced or what others — family, friends, or authority figures — told you. They can even come from what you read in books or the news, or on social media.

Everyone struggles with limiting beliefs. And we just seem to put up with them or tolerate them even though we subconsciously know they aren't serving us.

The Domino Effect

Limiting beliefs have a domino effect on other thoughts. You have a limiting belief, and the next thought that follows is even more limiting. The diminishing nature of the initial limiting belief seeps into each new thought, creating a snowball that gets bigger and bigger while you get smaller and smaller. "I'm not good at sales" starts rolling down the hill and suddenly becomes "I'm not good at talking to people," which then turns into "I am not good at what I do." That first limiting belief creates a slippery slope.

Limiting beliefs don't stay in the realm of *just thoughts* but morph into actions — or inaction. Because remember, your thoughts trigger how you feel, and those feelings are what fuel your actions, inactions, or reactions. When you think, "I can't afford to hire anyone to help with my business," or, "All the good help is taken," what actions follow? Do they create the business and the life you want?

Choose your thoughts with consciousness and care because they create your world. Limiting beliefs steal confidence and zap motivation. So why allow them to live inside your head and shape your reality?

FIND YOUR LIBERATING TRUTHS

Your limiting beliefs don't have to keep you in a box. You can trade them for liberating truths. In *Full Focus,*[6] Michael Hyatt shares ways to do that.

He suggests being mindful of when a thought is a belief (rather than a fact), and when you notice it, write it down. Keeping a record of your limiting beliefs over time can definitely help you see what's going on under the surface of your thoughts.

When you've written down your limiting belief, take a more in-depth look to determine whether it's helping or harming you. If it's helping you, great! But if not, you can *reject or reframe* it. According to Hyatt, if the belief is false, you can just reject it outright. An example of a limiting belief might be, "I'll never succeed in this market." That's just a false statement with no basis in fact. Unless you have special powers, you can't predict the future — and if you could, you'd use your powers to succeed.

Some limiting beliefs might be based on partial truth, which you need to recognize. In those cases, you can change the statement to reflect a more positive perspective. For instance, you might think, "I can't compete in the market because I don't have enough people working in my business." But until you take a closer look, you don't know what your resources are — so that statement may or may not be true. And even if it is, it's not necessarily a permanent obstacle. For instance, you could say, "To compete in my market, I need to offer these new services. Based on my data, I don't have the people to create a new service area immediately, but my team and I can work together to figure out what we can add for very little additional labor and create capital for the rest within the next two years." Now you've gone from a limiting belief to the beginning of a plan.

Once you've replaced the limiting belief with the new liberating truth, the final step is to start living in the *new truth*. Even if it feels strange or you don't quite believe it, keep saying it to yourself. Whenever the old belief pops into your head, you just follow the same process until it dissolves. I use these thought processes all the time when working through limiting beliefs with my clients.

No matter what your limiting belief is or what liberating truth you have adopted, there is one key ingredient you need in order to change and have the change stick. We'll talk about that in the next chapter. But here is your first clue — it's not an activity, and it only happens when you Think Big.

THINK BIGGER: YOUR LIMITING BELIEFS

1. Think about a problem you're dealing with. Write down all your thoughts about it — why you need to solve the problem, why you feel you can't or shouldn't, what is holding you back from taking action, etc. Make your thoughts as detailed as they need to be.

Now look at what you wrote and ask yourself a few questions.

2. Do my thoughts inspire me to move toward what is significant and valuable to me? Or are they keeping me stuck or moving me away from something of value? (I especially like this one because every thought you have is either taking you closer to or farther from your best self and your best life.)

3. Do my thoughts serve me? Are they useful?

4. If you answered NO to any of those questions, shift gears and attempt to shift each limiting belief into a liberating truth. What would be different if that liberating thought were true? (We'll talk more about this in a coming chapter.)

CHAPTER 4

BIG COMMITMENT: NARROW DOWN TO POWER UP

The path to success is to take massive, determined actions.

— Tony Robbins

COMMITTING TO EVERYTHING LEADS TO ACHIEVING NOTHING

*R*emember my client, Lindsey, who was doing everything? She was doing the work of several people — handling purchasing, talking to prospective major clients, overseeing inventory, and managing scheduling — and that was just in business. In her personal life, she still had to pick up kids from school, run errands, cook dinner, do all the things. And she knew that situation wasn't sustainable.

When you do everything, you don't do anything well. You don't have the time or mental energy to bring your best. After a while, it shows.

Once we took stock of *all the things*, she became very clear on what was important to her, and out of those important things, she became even clearer on what she wanted to commit to.

To get that clarity, we didn't use logic. We used feeling. A feeling can often drive your decision on whether to commit. Lindsey identified what she wanted to commit to by noticing whether it made her feel calm, cool, and collected. That was the feeling definer for her.

If it didn't give her that feeling, *it didn't make the list.* Period.

For example, she could easily commit to hiring help, both in her business and at home. While hiring help requires time and effort, the result — having more hands — created that feeling she craved. It gave her a sense of the light at the end of her tunnel of chaos.

With this purpose in mind, as well as a clear understanding of her goals (we'll talk about how to get that in later chapters), she could readily commit to actions that gave her more margin in her day and calm in her life.

WHY WE OVERCOMMIT

If your life resembles Lindsey's (or ever has before), you probably know overcommitment leads to burnout. Our thoughts are always spinning, and we have no place to park them. Nor do we know where to direct our energy and efforts.

How do we get to this place where we're overcommitted? Let's look at several potential reasons.

We allow fear to drive our actions. We fear letting others down, being seen as not caring or not doing enough, or actually not doing enough, leading to failure.

We logically believe we should. We have committed to the tasks/projects because, logically, they'll help us achieve our goals or because others will approve. They seem practical, or we feel obligated, but emotionally, we're not all-in. A commitment isn't a *should*. When most people say they're committed to something, it's only an intellectual commitment — it's not all-in. It sounds like a noble cause. It sounds like something they *should* be committed to.

We confuse being interested with being committed. When we're interested in something, it can seem important, but that doesn't mean it's committed-level important. This confusion is one of the biggest reasons people take on way too many obligations, so let's look at it in more depth.

THE DIFFERENCE BETWEEN INTERESTED AND COMMITTED

I am not going to lie: This morning, I did not want to work out.

I worked out anyway.

I didn't want to take my daughter to get her wisdom teeth extracted at 7:00 a.m.

I got up and took her anyway.

I didn't want to do billing and invoicing.

I did it anyway.

Why? Because I said I was going to do those things. I said I would do them because I was, and still am, all-in with their results. I want to be fit, and I want my kids to be healthy. I want to get paid, and I want to do all the other things I'm doing because I know they'll lead to big results for me in some way.

There is a HUGE difference between being committed versus just being interested.

When you're interested in something, you like the idea of the thing. You're curious about it. You want to explore it and learn about it, but you're not necessarily ready to give it your whole attention. It hasn't yet convinced you it's important enough to take over a large part of your resources.

When you're committed, you feel wholeheartedly dedicated and loyal to a cause, activity, person, or job.

Wholeheartedly dedicated. I love that. That is ALL-IN, intellectually, physically, emotionally, and spiritually.

When you're really, truly committed, you're ready to do whatever it takes to achieve the result. Whether or not you love the activity you're doing to achieve it doesn't matter. When you're committed, your desire for the result, not your love for the activity, drives you to do the activity.

Our brains like to think that anything we're interested in should be important, and we should put resources toward it.

WHEN YOU'RE **COMMITTED,** YOUR DESIRE FOR THE RESULT, NOT YOUR LOVE FOR THE ACTIVITY, **DRIVES YOU** TO DO THE ACTIVITY.

Interested	Committed
Long-term relationship	Married
Complain about not enough work	Ask for the job
Feel like there is never enough time	Delegate
Debate about whether my child should play soccer	Sign up for soccer

FREE UP YOUR ENERGY FOR YOUR REAL COMMITMENTS

My client Claire was interested in creating a course. She wanted to sell it and share her valuable knowledge with other practice owners in her industry to have a source of passive income. It was a win-win. She invested in the idea, hiring an expert in course creation to help her, and she even started putting together the content.

However, every time she coached with me, she brought up the course as a problem. "I know I really need to spend some time on it. The course creator isn't very communicative. And I think that is what is holding me back. She's not holding me accountable."

So, I suggested we set some deadlines together. Claire continued to create content, albeit slowly. But I noted whenever she brought up the course in our sessions, her voice grew dull, and it sounded like she was talking about doing chores.

After six months, I finally suggested that she abandon the project. This brought a flurry of emotion to the table.

"I have done so much work. I have invested time, money, and brain power. I could never abandon this. It would all seem like such a waste. Let alone not making any money from it or putting forth the value I bring to this industry into the world."

I acknowledged she was definitely interested in this project. It did have potential. But she wasn't committed and all-in with making it happen. She was putting resources toward it, but that was all. She wasn't putting *committed energy* toward it; she was just putting *interested energy* toward it. By just giving it interested energy, she was doing it and herself a disservice. She was giving energy to it, but not enough to really make a difference. That project was also *taking resources — including energy — away* from other things that felt more important to her, to which she could truly commit.

Before she could throw in the towel, Claire had to get to a place of feeling neutral about it. At first, she just wanted to let go because she was desperate to feel relieved. But feeling relieved is always temporary.

So, she switched her thinking, going back to one of the original purposes of the course — creating income. She decided that rather than doing the course, she would change the structure of her pricing and offerings.

She also had to realize the course wasn't a waste of her time, even if she wasn't finishing it. She had learned a lot through the work thus far. She could always pick it up later. Perhaps what she had done would morph into something even more valuable if given committed energy in the future.

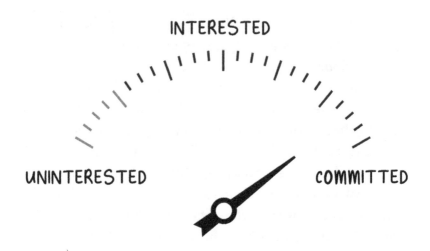

Four Questions to Find Your Commitment Level

Do you have projects you just can't seem to move forward but you can't let go of? Here are some questions to ask to see whether you're truly committed to them.

1. **Do I tend to focus on all the obstacles to doing this activity, or am I focused on achieving the result?** If you're focused on obstacles, you're looking for reasons not to do the activity. You may need to do some other mindset work to uncover fears or other things hampering your commitment, and you may want to see if you can do something different to solve the problem this activity is meant to solve.

2. **How do I feel when I can't get to this activity?** Do I feel anxious and seek to get back on track, or do I easily set it aside for tomorrow? If you feel anxious about not doing the activity, it's probably a higher priority.

3. **When someone asks me why I haven't done it, what do I tell them?** The answers you give show what you're prioritizing over this activity. These are the things you're choosing to do rather than the thing you say you want to do — this is a clear sign you're not committed.

4. **Am I waiting to be motivated to do this activity?** If you're not motivated, you're not committed. However, if you expect to enjoy every part of this activity, that's a false assumption. You may not like going to the gym and sweating on the elliptical, but if you're committed to the results, you'll still be there every day.

EXTRAORDINARY COMMITMENT FUELS BIG RESULTS

Imagine what your life would be like if you actually lived up to your commitments. ALL of them.

What kind of relationship would you have with your significant other?

What kind of relationship would you have with the people you serve?

What kind of opportunities would you create for yourself?

How would that make you feel about yourself?

I venture to say, from experience, the answers to those questions will be, "Awesome."

"Ugh," you might think. "I'm already overcommitted. Now you're asking me to be extraordinarily committed? That would be exhausting!"

That's a limiting belief based on assumptions — and ironically, those assumptions are why you're currently over-committed and exhausted. What I mean by Extraordinary Commitment is the ability to commit to achieving extraordinary results — which means being smart about your commitments in the first place.

To *wholeheartedly dedicate* yourself to things, you must be very choosy about what you dedicate yourself to.

And you're not doing it just for you. Overcommitment leads to misery for you and everyone you're involved with. You cannot possibly bring your full gifts and talents to the table when you're overcommitted.

One of my favorite sayings is, "You have reasons, or you have results."

Choose results.

Choose to be **extraordinary** at a few things by being truly committed versus being good'nuff at everything because you're overcommitted.

Being fully committed doesn't mean committing to everything — it means knowing what to commit to and what to take a pass on.

Thinking this way about commitment affects every area of your life. Here are just some of the benefits.

Extraordinary Commitment gives you energy. These commitments don't zap your energy. They aren't chores. Doing what you're truly emotionally invested in generates more energy, no matter how challenging or difficult it is.

Extraordinary Commitment saves time. The land of indecision not only uses a lot of energy but also wastes time. "I don't know" keeps us in Limbo Land and postpones progress. It sends us to Busy Land, where we can cross things off the list without achieving anything important. And besides, not deciding is a decision — a decision to *just* stay interested. It gives us a sense that we're doing something without actually accomplishing it. And what that really means is you have decided to STAY in a place of confusion, doubt, and fear instead of making a decision that will lead to progress.

Extraordinary Commitment increases your action. If your purpose is meaningful and will contribute positively to the world, then you have a responsibility to make decisions. By hesitating, you reduce your contribution. This even relates to working out or staying healthy in general. When we're healthier, we contribute in a more meaningful way — we become 100 percent contributors.

COMMITMENT = DECISION

Commitment is really a form of decision-making. Decision-making is power over one's life. By exercising that power and being disciplined about your commitments, you make life interesting and create growth.

Extraordinary Commitment goes a step further. Big Thinkers don't make arbitrary decisions. They make clear ones that lead them further toward fulfilling their purpose *and* their emotional needs, and they choose wisely, making sure they are investing their mental, physical, time, and relationship resources into the most rewarding and fulfilling

NOT DECIDING IS A DECISION — A DECISION TO **JUST** STAY INTERESTED.

commitments. They are as clear about what not to commit to as they are about what to commit to.

Decisions Lead to Action

Until we make a decision, we don't take action. Making the decision gives you the power to take action because you're now committed rather than hovering between options.

Decision	Action
YES, I am going to create time for myself.	Hire the trainer instead of training the team myself.
YES, I am going to move.	Purchase a new property.
YES, I am going to make $1M this year.	Ask the prospect for the sale.

The same can be said for the decision of NO. Even a NO creates movement — just in a different direction.

Decision	Action
NO, I am not going to move.	Learn to love this place even more.
NO, I am not going on a trip.	Have fun at home.
NO, I am not investing in new equipment.	Maximize what I have.

Only when we make the decision can we start taking action — and only by taking action do we show up in a much better way. Without decision — which is really just a committed feeling — we remain powerless to take action. The thought, "I can do this," leads to actually doing it. Remember:

Thoughts → Feelings → Actions → Results.

Without the committed feeling a decision brings, the action doesn't happen.

I see this in my clients when they decide to work with a coach and sign on the dotted line. Even before our first official coaching session, the growth they experience is more than they have experienced in the last several years because by deciding to work with a coach, they have committed to working on themselves.

A Simple Decision Can Change Everything

My client Diane is an artist. One of her problems was that she suffered from extreme creative blocks. She loved painting, but for some reason, she couldn't seem to do it anymore. She had sold ten works, so her issue was a mystery to her.

However, when we began our sessions, something she told me puzzled me.

She'd never told anyone she was an artist or that she had sold ten paintings. She had sold them privately through a mutual friend and signed them with a fictitious name, so no one but that person and her spouse knew — not even her best friend.

She hadn't said anything because she feared being an artist wasn't a worthy profession and painting all day was frivolous. She believed her first role should always be mother and spouse, not painter.

So, she hid. Fear prevented her from just saying, "I'm an artist, and my job is important."

Her creativity recognized where she was — living in the land of *interested*, not *committed*. She was interested in partnering with her creativity, but she didn't want to make the relationship public. Since she was telling her creativity it wasn't important, it responded by not showing up when she wanted it to. After all, why show up if it didn't matter?

It was forcing her to make a choice, and she was getting the uncomfortable message, loud and clear.

Finally, she had a revelation. "If this is meant to be a career — if I am meant to be a painter — wouldn't just CALLING myself an artist (i.e., a creative person) lead to more action?" she asked. "Wouldn't I be painting more often? And wouldn't I figure out a way to make it part of my life?"

The answer was YES.

Either she was an artist, or she wasn't. Either it was important, or it wasn't. Either she was painting, or she wasn't painting. And she decided, "YES, I am a painter — and painters paint. And that part of me is important."

And with that, her creative block dissipated, and she began painting again.

It's time to clear out the confusion and decide. What do you really want to commit to? What would be possible if you did commit? And then commit. All-in. No excuses.

It's time to be extraordinary.

COMMIT TO BEING
EXTRAORDINARILY COMMITTED

Imagine happily living up to all your commitments because you've carefully selected exactly which ones you want to do. You're now Extraordinarily Committed versus overcommitted. You're not tied to things you aren't all-in on, so nothing is sucking your energy from the priorities you've set for yourself.

What would life look like? Here are several real-life examples.

Arianna: Finding a Niche Draws All the Right Clients

My client Arianna is an award-winning photographer and a skilled videographer. When she started her business, she knew she could serve anyone who needed photos or video — commercial or private.

She feared that by tying herself down to only one type of customer or medium, she would be missing out on a lot of business. And even targeting one medium could be problematic because commercial clients — particularly marketing agencies who are providing content for print and digital formats, including social media, often want both photo and video content.

But doing both photo and video well is challenging for one person. And being a generalist created issues. She couldn't market effectively to such a broad audience, and she often didn't even know what to market or how. After a few sessions, she took a leap of faith, deciding to serve one audience (just marketing agencies, particularly those with deep social media expertise) with one product (photography). It would create both the focus and a flow she craved in her business. It would give her the freedom to do even better work in the photo arena. Once she had truly committed, she was all-in.

Although directing all efforts toward one audience with just one product took initial effort, after just one year of establishing her niche, she was more profitable than ever, and her calendar was filled a year in advance.

Lindsey: Delegation Doubles Profit and Creates Confidence

Remember Lindsey? Her furniture boutique did very well in her region, with lots of repeat high-end customers. Its side branch, which handled furnishing and accessorizing model homes for several regional home builders, was also doing well.

But Lindsey was handling the model homes herself, which required onsite trips to assess needs. She didn't have the time or energy to do everything, and she really enjoyed sales and interacting with her customers all day.

Unfortunately, eliminating model home furnishing from her business would remove a sizable revenue center and good exposure for her business.

She sorted through the possibilities, deciding to stay in-store to handle sales and display design, where she preferred to be, and hiring help that she would lead and manage to handle the other things — namely, purchasing supplies and furnishing the model homes.

By narrowing her commitments, she doubled her profit in one year, tamed much of her chaos, grew her confidence in her business, and increased her sense of calm at home.

Tamara: Streamlining Efficiency Leads to New Growth

My client Tamara, an accountant and business owner, managed a team of 25 alongside doing her own work. She knew she needed to revamp, but until we started pulling apart the responsibilities in her organization, she didn't realize how many people were handling overlapping responsibilities. This led to duplicated efforts, inefficiency, and wasted resources.

Changing the situation meant restructuring the company. She was interested in doing this, but moving to a commitment was hard and would take time she believed she didn't have. She had to step out of her own comfort zone to tell people what to do in a whole new way. That felt scary.

We created an accountability chart, which isn't an organizational chart but rather a chart documenting who is responsible for what and ensuring there is one owner or responsible party for each job or task. As we did, Tamara realized that resources (including time – bonus!) opened up if only one person was responsible for each project. This knowledge made the changes much easier. The team had been asking for more resources — (time, money, and brain power). This reorganization could make that happen *without* adding things into the firm.

Tamara committed to the entire process, ensuring the company adhered to its new accountability chart. As a result, the firm boosted its efficiency, its people were much happier, and they could now tackle the projects that had been on the back burner forever.

So, what are you ready to decide on? Are you willing to move from interested to committed? What will happen if you do? Let's go!

We've tackled all your mindset issues — your fear, your limiting beliefs, and your indecisiveness. You're powered up and ready to move into the next phase of Thinking Big. This is the fun part because it's time to start planning your life the way you really want it.

THINK BIGGER: MAKE THAT DECISION!

1. Identify one challenge or situation you need (or want!) to move forward on but just can't seem to take that next step.

2. Using the four questions in this chapter, find your commitment level. Are you interested or committed?

3. If you're interested, do you even want to be committed? If so, what would it take to get to commitment? And what would you gain or what would change if you were committed?

4. If you're committed, then what is holding you back from moving forward and deciding the next best steps? Is it fear or something else? Message me on social media (see my About the Author page) or email me at Andrea@AndreaLiebross.com and tell me about it!

If you're still hesitating on the decision, keep reading, and think about it more as we go. As you read more, you may get more ideas for the best way to think about this decision.

PART TWO

PLANS

Set Your Destination

CHAPTER 5

BIG PICTURE: WHAT'S YOUR REAL SITUATION?

All problems become smaller when you confront them instead of dodging them.

— **William F. Halsey**

When you make plans to go on a trip, you must know your current location, where you're going, and the route you plan to take.

When making your Big Plan — the next destination for your life and business — it's no different. You must understand four things:

- Where you currently sit in the areas you'll be planning for (business, life, relationships, etc.). This is Point A, your Current Location on your GPS.
- Where you want to go in those areas — what does the next "you" look like? This is Point B.
- Why you want to go there — this is your fuel.
- The best way to get there — what are your stops along the way to Point B?

GETTING TO THE TRUE STORY

When I start working with a client, we examine the facts of her situation so we can get a sense of where she is. This is the Point A I mentioned above.

This process can reveal a lot — not just about the facts, but about what they are thinking and feeling.

When I suggested to Lindsey that we look at her financial data to see how she was managing her resources, she didn't seem very enthusiastic.

"Ugh," she said. "Do we have to?"

"Why don't you want to?" I asked, surprised.

She sighed. "It makes me want to vomit."

I was a bit taken aback. After all, she had already told me finances were a major headache for her.

But we had to get past this internal block to get anywhere. We needed to look at the data to get some insights into what was going on — what was working and what wasn't working. It's a snapshot in time.

It's like in the movie *National Lampoon's European Vacation* when the family gets stuck on a roundabout. They just keep driving in circles because they can't get over to the exit lane. Something always gets in their way. Each time around the circle, the dad tries to point out the scenery to stay positive. But after the 55th time, it's not really exciting anymore.

Lindsey was circling on her own roundabout, and it was just as frustrating.

She was making decisions from her gut, and many weren't achieving the desired results. What she needed to do was make decisions from the data, which would show her the facts on how she was managing her resources.

She wasn't taking the time to examine the data because she didn't have time to do it.

She didn't have the time because she was already doing too many other things.

She was doing too many other things because she didn't want to delegate tasks to any other people.

She didn't want to delegate tasks to other people because she feared it might not be the best use of their time (that she was paying for) or her time in explaining what needed to be delegated.

She feared it might not be the best use of time because she didn't know the total resources available.

She didn't know the total resources available because she didn't want to look at her financial data or track her time.

And she feared looking at any data because she was managing things from her gut, and she was afraid of what the data would show her.

And so it went, around and around in a circle, moving but getting nowhere. ("Look kids! Big Ben! Parliament!")[7]

To get off the roundabout, Lindsey needed the data. From it, she could make better decisions based on facts versus decisions based on her gut.

So, after a little probing, we got to the heart of her disgust.

"I feel like I'm back in school," she confessed. "It's like getting a test grade. Either I'm passing the course or failing. If the financial numbers are bad, it means I'm bad at what I do. Ugh! I don't need that on top of everything else."

Aha! Now we're getting somewhere.

As we talked, she realized how crucial it was for her to shift her mindset.

TAKING A SITUATIONAL SNAPSHOT

When I do a situational Snapshot, it's a well-rounded approach. Here are some tools I use with clients to get this information:

- The Seven Facets Assessment evaluates the seven different dimensions of their lives, including business and personal aspects.
- A Seven Facets Relationship exercise assesses their relationship with each of the facets.
- A Mental House exercise discovers what's going on in their minds.

How clients *think and feel* about the facts often doesn't match up with the *actual* facts — the truths provable in a court of law. As in Lindsey's case, their limiting beliefs prevent them from seeing the liberating truths within the actual facts.

We often substitute our own opinions or assumptions for facts without even thinking about it. Suppose you think you need to change things by hiring more people — at home or in your business. Without knowing the facts, that may or may be true. But when we look at the facts, we might see that you actually have too many people doing the wrong things or that you really don't need to hire more. You need to streamline your services and start functioning more efficiently.

Figure 5.1 The Success Triangle

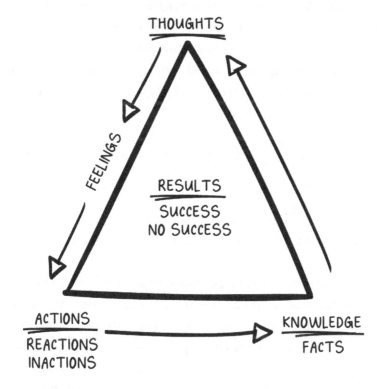

Facts trigger thoughts, and thoughts lead to feelings. Feelings trigger you to act/react (or not act) in certain ways. These actions become new facts, which create more thoughts. This cycle can create positive results/ success or negative results/no success — it all depends on the quality of the thoughts and beliefs you put into it.

NUMBERS TALK, BUT YOU PICK THEIR STORY

In Lindsey's situation, assessing her numbers was just an opportunity to evaluate **where she was** with the business so she could use data to decide her next steps. She didn't have to label those numbers, and they didn't have to label her. They truly were just numbers.

The problem was that she was tying them to her self-worth. "I should be doing better" or "I should be better" are thoughts but not facts. Those thoughts created feelings she didn't like, causing her to avoid looking at the facts entirely.

But once Lindsey started looking at the data differently, the whole picture changed.

Fact #1: Good news! She was creating revenue! That's a great fact.

Fact #2: Most of her revenue was coming from certain income streams. The numbers showed her which ones these were.

Fact #3: Some of her services were more profitable than others. The numbers allowed her to see which ones. With these facts, she could eliminate some of the tiny dribs and drabs of revenue and focus on the big drivers. That created some space. With that new focus, she could see where to reallocate resources — time, money, other people, and brain power.

Fact #4: A whopping 80 percent of her business was coming from 20 percent of her clients. This knowledge prompted her to create some VIP clients, allowing her to focus even more and free up additional resources.

But that wasn't the whole picture. She also needed to look at her projections — all her ongoing projects and what was on deck. When she did that, she remembered more money was coming in next week and month. The picture got clearer.

She also found some other potential revenue streams she hadn't even considered. She had options to choose from when running her future projects. She could Think Bigger — beyond what was happening in the present. She could increase business without hustling. She found hidden profits and time.

She didn't even see the potential for more profit until she paused and looked and started to become friends with her data, versus feeling like the numbers were the enemy she had to hide from.

The Rest of Lindsey's Snapshot

We gathered much more than financial data. After examining the rest of the information, Lindsey saw she had some staffing issues. She had to make some decisions about whom to keep and whom to let go, and that made her uncomfortable. She always wanted to make sure everybody felt great about working with her, for her, and with clients. Letting people go was the best solution, but that didn't make it easy.

However, having the wrong person in the wrong job (or seat) is like putting a square peg in a round hole — training really wouldn't help, and it was unlikely they would succeed in their roles. She realized some of these people didn't even want to be doing the things she was assigning them. She had to have some very honest conversations.

The honest conversations were eye-opening. When she saw a red flag in the past, she tended to hesitate and shy away from it. But now, with the shift in her own self-concept as a leader, she was more inclined to address issues ahead of time and not be so reactive, especially when it came down to people.

She also realized where she needed to outsource rather than try to train people in-house, which saved her a lot of money.

The data gave her what she needed, not only to understand what was going on but to affect the outcome. It gave her a starting point — but she got to pick how the story ended. And that meant choosing a happy ending overall, though she had to go through some challenges along the way.

PAUSING TO THINK IS STRATEGIC

We're programmed to be reactive — to defend. Back to the motivational triad again — we're reactive by nature (trying to protect ourselves) and love to operate on automatic pilot (much more efficient). And those two modes work when we're trying to get everything done and keep all the balls rolling.

But by taking a Snapshot, we move out of reactive and out of automatic pilot. We can allow for what I call a Strategic Pause. This is where the magic happens.

This often happens naturally when clients engage in coaching. Finally, they give themselves some margin. It creates space on their calendars to think. Coaching gives them the permission they wouldn't give themselves otherwise. One of the many roles a coach serves is as an accountability partner, so if they're not doing the work, they are letting down their coach — and themselves.

TAKE YOUR OWN SNAPSHOT

Assess Your Seven Facets

It is only when we understand where you are that we can start to create change, and you can be more responsible for creating that change. So, it's time to get a sense of where you're at.

We need to pull the curtain back on how you're feeling or your level of satisfaction in all facets of life. This is a version of the assessment I go through with new clients to get an idea of where they are in their own Big Picture.

Assess your current level of satisfaction on a scale of 1 to 10 in each of these Seven Life Facets. A 10 would be "Amazing; nothing needs to change. I am really happy where I'm at." A 1 would be "Horrible; I don't even want to think about that area of life."

_____ **Time:** How are you using your time? Do you feel like you never have enough time? Or plenty of time? Are you using your time on the things that are most important to you? Does your use of time align with your priorities?

_____ **Systems and Processes:** Do you have systems and processes in both your personal life and your business/professional life? If you have systems, do you use them? Are they working for you? Do they make things easier and more efficient? Or do you follow them for a week and then forget about them for a while?

_____ **Relationships:** What do your relationships look like? Your relationship with yourself and your relationship with other people — friends, family, colleagues, and your team? Who are you spending your time with? And is that someone you want to be spending time with? Do you give the people you care about enough time?

—— **Finances:** How do you feel about your finances? Do you cringe every time you look at your bank account? Do you worry about saving for retirement? Do you wish you had a budget? And if you do have a budget, do you follow it? How do you use it? In your business, do you understand your cash flow? Do you want to invest in your business but are afraid you don't have the money? And do you often wonder where all the money goes?

—— **Business:** What is your level of satisfaction with your business? Is it giving you what you want it to give you? Does it become consuming? Or are you able to separate it from your own identity? Do you still enjoy being a business owner? Are you having fun?

—— **Health and Wellness:** What is your level of satisfaction with your own health and wellness? Do you move your body? Do you get enough sleep? Are you eating the food that fuels your body? When was the last time you had a checkup at the doctor? Do you get to the dentist regularly?

—— **Recreation:** How do you spend your free time? Do you have free time? Do you have interests or avocational pursuits or hobbies that aren't related to your work or your family? Do you still play?

I'm guessing you didn't give yourself a 10 in every category. There's probably a smattering of 4s and 6s and 8s. Maybe even a 5.5 or a 1.

For every Life Facet that isn't a 10, ask yourself, "What would have to change in order for me to give a 10 to this facet?" What is THE problem? Is there one? Should you spend more time on this facet? Change the way you think about things? Readjust your expectations? Probably all of those things. Examine each facet and write down what you need to make it a 10.

Now, look at each Life Facet again. What's at stake if you don't get it to a 10? What is it costing you being where you're right now in that category? Write that down, too.

Third, examine the facet with the highest stakes, the most potential cost. Most people tell me their mental health is the one that has the greatest stakes. Even before they bring up money. Their mental health, their well-being is most important. Whatever yours is, think about this question: If it was a 10, what would that allow you to do? What would be different? Write that down, too.

And finally, look at all Seven Life Facets as a whole. What does your wheel look like? Do some of your facets have low scores (thus, short spokes), while others have very high scores (so, long spokes)? If your wheel is too lopsided, it's good to look at the really low scores as potential priorities — especially if they could affect everything else. For instance, if your health is a short spoke, that's probably going to cause issues in the other areas. If you're not feeling well, you won't be on your game and able to show up as your best self for your family, your clients, or you. Your relationships may suffer. You won't be able to create the revenue you want. You'll be spending money on medical care. One facet can definitely impact others.

Now you have the beginning of your Snapshot. But let's look deeper.

Relationships: Your Seven Life Facets as People

This exercise can really illuminate your situation because it takes you out of your head and lets you explore how things feel. It puts you in creative mode wearing a different set of glasses.

Think about each Life Facet as if it were a person, and you have a relationship with that person.

If your time were a person, what would it look like? Describe it. Would it be a jittery, bad-tempered old Scrooge-like miser who wants to control your life and money, with whom you're always fighting? Would it be a little kid running around blowing bubbles and playing hopscotch, who you're always trying to corral into doing homework?

It is powerful to think about your business as if it were a person. Who is it? What is your relationship with this person (your business)? Is it a demanding, critical aunt you don't like to talk to except when you have to? Is it a little kid you have to babysit all the time? Is it a respected peer with interesting thoughts and ideas whom you enjoy being around? Is it a fun but not very serious romantic engagement that you're just dabbling in?

Is it your grandma? It will always be there for you, no matter what? Is it an old friend who you only talk to or see a few times a year — you can leave it alone but then pick up exactly where you left off? It is your roommate — you co-exist but don't love each other? Is it an authority figure in a social organization — maybe a church official or someone similar — it expects you to show up out of duty?

Your Mind as a House: A Mental Snapshot

When you're thinking small, you're lost in details and trivia that eat up your day. These details create mental clutter.

That's why your Snapshot isn't complete without an inventory of your mental spaces. What are you storing in your mind?

I love Brooke Castillo's way of thinking about the mind as a "Mental House."[8] (And no, I don't mean a mental institution, though sometimes it could certainly feel that way!) We can look at our minds as a set of rooms where certain things live or are stored. In our physical houses, we declutter, organize, and remodel to make our spaces more useful and welcoming for ourselves. Decluttering gets rid of old stuff to help free up space for the things we need. Organizing helps us keep things in logical, accessible places so we can find them quickly, and we know at a glance when we need resources because similar things are grouped in one place. Remodeling helps change the structure and use of our house in a major way, so the floor plan suits our needs as we change.

It's useful to think of your mind as your internal home — a bunch of rooms decorated and stocked with your thoughts and feelings.

You might find a lot of things as you walk through your mental house. Here are some things to look out for.

Past versions of you. These are all your ideas about yourself throughout your life — as a child at various ages, as a teenager just starting out, and all the stages in between. You have thoughts and feelings attached to each version of you. The Past Yous personify moments of awkwardness you'd like to forget and moments of achievement you're proud of. As you look around, which moments do you see the most — ones you're proud of or ones you're embarrassed about? When guests come over, do you tell any Past Yous to go into the closet and not come out till the guests leave? Why? Some of these ideas may give you clues to subconscious ideas you picked up in the past. These are still potentially driving your decisions without you even knowing.

Ideas. These are all the things you'd like to try, do, or create. Look around and notice what kinds of ideas are here and how they're organized. Are the ideas all over the place? Are they organized well? Are there any crazy ones? Are there any exciting ones you want to commit to right away?

> *We need an invention like X.*
> *If we create a new service, it should have X, Y, and Z qualities.*
> *I want to make new friends.*
> *I should open a coffee shop!*
> *We should move to a new office.*
> *I want to participate on the board of X organization.*

Does seeing all your ideas together inspire and excite you, or does it overwhelm you?

Opinions. This "room" includes your opinions about yourself (including your Past Yous) and other people. These can be positive or negative. You may even find your Frenemy in one of the rooms, stocking the mental shelves with negative judgments about you.

What kinds of opinions live here? Are they rigid, flexible, positive, negative? Are they supporting you or undermining you? Do any need to be more closely examined?

Gratitude. Gratitude isn't just a feeling; it's the act of valuing and loving something or someone and goes beyond feeling or opinion. For instance, I can like a pair of sneakers, but that doesn't mean I am deeply grateful for them and treat them with reverence. On the other hand, I can have a temporary negative opinion (thought and feeling) of how my loved one acts, but that doesn't change the fact that I am grateful for and love that person.

In your Mental House, you may find things you're grateful for — the things you think about on a regular basis that bring out positive emotions in you. These are the things you want to keep in your current life — things you cherish. I hope you have listed yourself as one of these things.

Look around your house and find 10 things you appreciate about yourself. What are 10 things you're great at? Appreciation — whether it's appreciating yourself or others or just your situation in general — creates more energy. When you carry gratitude, it's difficult to fill your house's rooms with negative thoughts. And when you're having a tough day, gratitude is a great friend to hang out with for a while.

CREATE THE NEXT SNAPSHOT: MENTAL DECLUTTERING

Big Thinkers use their brains to achieve Big Results. We don't waste energy on clutter and things that don't serve us. We also get to choose how our Mental Houses are organized and laid out.

How is your Mental House serving you? Is it big enough to hold the Future You that's coming — the one who will have a Big Plan? Think about that as you redesign. Maybe you'll need a bigger house to serve your needs or cheerier-looking furniture that will invite more positive thoughts. You might want to add entire new rooms and floors to hold all your exciting ideas.

Thinking Big is also being smart about what you allow into your mind. You have the power to control that — no one else does. You get to decide whether to bring something into your mental space or not based on whether you need it or not.

That brings up one last thing: Don't let *anyone else* put anything in your house you don't want — especially in the Room of Subconscious Thoughts. If someone — a friend, a client, an advertisement, the news media — tries to give you a thought gift that will just become another piece of clutter, now you'll be aware of it, and you can kindly but firmly say, "No, thank you. I don't need that in my house." You don't even have to say it to their face; you can just set it out for the *mental trash* when they aren't looking. You don't need to blindly accept every thought that comes your way.

Journal to Keep a Clean Mental House

You may notice things in your Mental House that you want to remove or change. By keeping a journal and doing frequent inventory, you'll be able to manage this process better.

You'll be surprised how this works. After a while, looking at your journal will be like talking to a good friend who is there to support you and doesn't try to talk down to you.

That good friend is you.

Now that we have a Snapshot and we know what's in your Mental House, let's do some more in-depth sorting so we can create our new situation. We'll do that in the next chapter.

THINK BIGGER: YOUR SNAPSHOT

1. Refer back to the Assess Your Seven Life Facets section in this chapter and answer the questions to create your own snapshot.

2. When you visualized the Seven Facets as people, what qualities about these people are affecting your relationships with them? Are these relationships working for you, and if not, what needs to change?

3. What thoughts from your Mental House are getting in the way of you taking each facet to a 10?

4. If each facet was a 10, how would you feel? What would be possible in your life and business?

CHAPTER 6

BIG DECISIONS: UNTANGLE THE KNOTS

Until you are clear nothing will be.
The moment you are clear everything will be.

— Rasheed Ogunlaru

WHY ARE YOU STUCK?

If you followed the exercises in the last chapter and put together your own Snapshot of facts, thoughts, and feelings, you probably already realize your thoughts are the biggest things holding you back. Some may be obvious, but others might still be a puzzle.

One of the hardest things to do when you're on a roundabout is to get off the roundabout. You can't necessarily figure out the thought that's keeping you from turning down the road you want to get on because it's hidden in all the other thought traffic you're dealing with. Plus, it's scary to try to get off the roundabout. You have to maneuver in a direction that traffic doesn't want to let you go in. Accidents can happen. And you might get off at the wrong place and end up going who knows where. Maybe staying on the roundabout is easier.

That's why women benefit from having a coach who isn't embedded in their thinking and can see not only what and where the client is circling but why. To understand what's going on, you have to follow your thoughts through all their twists and turns.

Tangled Priorities Prevent Progress

I often think of the situation as a bunch of tangled balls of yarn. All the different strings have wound together to make a big knot. Each type of yarn represents our thoughts and decisions about one of the Seven Life Facets. Nothing is sorted out, and because they're all tangled together, they prevent any real progress. You can't use any of the yarn to do anything until you untangle the knots and separate each piece.

But it's hard to untie them. You can't move one thing because five other things are wrapped around it. Sometimes the knots are so tight you have to coax them loose with great patience.

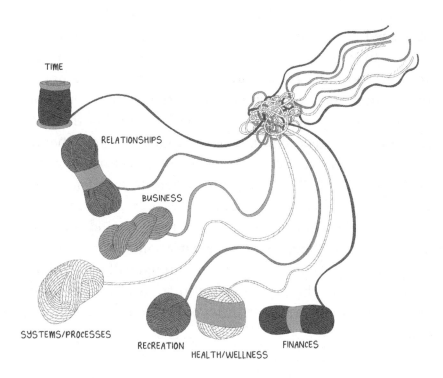

TIME

RELATIONSHIPS

BUSINESS

SYSTEMS/PROCESSES

RECREATION

HEALTH/WELLNESS

FINANCES

However, it's worth doing because untangling our minds helps us:

- Determine what skeins of yarn we want to use (the facet or facets we want to work on and the related priorities or projects we want to tackle).
- Decide which other facets we want to put on the shelf right now so they don't get tangled with the current projects. These could be facets we're happy with right now, or they're not as high a priority as others.

Think back to the Parking Lot you're stuck in. What's happened is that each time you've focused on a priority, you've done the equivalent of plugging a destination into your mental GPS. But before you start on your journey to that destination, you turn your attention to another priority and plug in a new destination without erasing the first. If you have plugged multiple destinations into your mental GPS, and they are located in different directions, you get nowhere. Your GPS doesn't know where to take you. Then add the crazy fact that sometimes we plug in destinations we don't even realize we're deciding to go to, and you have another layer of complexity and frustration.

In this chapter, we're going to untangle all your priorities. But before that, we're going to transform your limiting beliefs into liberating truths so they don't keep hanging you up.

FROM LIMITING BELIEFS TO LIBERATING TRUTHS

In previous chapters, we've talked about how fear can hide in the shadows and cause you to stagnate or do things that don't support your goals. You get stuck.

Remember the crazy fact that sometimes you have a fear — but you don't know it? Fear is a feeling, so it comes from a thought, remember? Thoughts lead to feelings. Limiting beliefs are thoughts that can create fear.

We discussed limiting beliefs already, but let's take a deeper dive into five common beliefs that coaches see over and over and examine how to change them.[9]

Five Common Limiting Beliefs and Liberating Truths	
LIMITING BELIEF	**LIBERATING TRUTH**
I'm not enough. (Impostor Syndrome)	I am enough. I KNOW EXACTLY WHAT I AM DOING.
I'm not good enough. (Perfectionism)	I am good enough. THE SERVICE/PRODUCT I GIVE OUR CLIENTS IS ALWAYS EXCELLENT.
I'm just not doing enough. (Hyper-achievement)	It is enough. I'M DOING PLENTY.
There aren't enough. (Scarcity)	There are enough. THERE ARE PLENTY OF PROSPECTIVE CLIENTS OUT THERE.
I'm not ready. (Fear of Success)	I'm ready right now. LET'S GO!

Limiting Belief #1: "I'm Not Enough" (Impostor Syndrome)

Impostor syndrome happens to almost everyone in some way. But it's just another limiting belief. As an entrepreneur, it can be career-stifling.

This belief keeps people stuck. They stay in situations they don't like because, deep inside, they feel they don't have what it takes to change the situation. When I ask people if they have evidence that their limiting belief might NOT be true, 99 percent of the time, they say YES. But they forget about that evidence. That's why even people who have already proven themselves can still have this limiting belief.

Remember Tamara, who was a successful accounting firm owner with a team of 25 and 400 clients a year? She wanted to serve even more clients, scale up her business, and mentor her team. In one session, she told me, "I was really scared, and that's when my impostor syndrome kicked in. I thought, 'I can't do this; who do I think I am? I'm not that good as a business owner. I'm just an accountant.' But clearly, I could if I already had all those clients and my team and three locations."

Moving out of your comfort zone is scary. Even when you have the skills you need to do it, your fear will tell you that you don't. That's your Frenemy, keeping you safe.

Liberating Truth: "I am enough. I know EXACTLY what I am doing, and I am constantly learning and growing."

Limiting Belief #2: "It's Not Good Enough" (Perfectionism)

Perfectionism creates a fear of making mistakes outside the comfort zone. It causes you to try to be perfect in the eyes of others, keeping you from pursuing what you want for fear of what they would think. Or, it can keep you stuck resenting others, thinking they aren't doing things well enough or how you would do them. You don't realize you're the real issue.

Arianna's initial perfectionism with her two new photographers negatively impacted her business. "I was so nitpicky about how they approached their photo shoots," she recalled. "I had to realize they brought their own creative perspectives to the work, and we all could learn from each other. Once I accepted that, I welcomed their ideas, and we tried lots of new things to keep our work fresh. As a result, we started blowing away our competitors, and our business has tripled."

Arianna worked hard to calm her reactivity and develop self-awareness. She has grown as a person and improved her leadership approach. She delegates more to her small but growing team, trusting they can handle what she's sending their way. And since she's stepped back and let them make more decisions, they have more opportunities to grow and to build their own skills.

Liberating Truth: "It isn't only good enough, it's GREAT. And it's improving every day!"

Limiting Belief #3: "I'm Just Not Doing Enough" (Hyper-Achievement)

Hyper-achievers often look like they're on top of the world as they reach goal after goal. The problem is that they depend on constant achievement for self-validation. They barely notice each success because they're already focused on the next one. Often, they suffer from burnout.

I struggle with hyper-achievement myself. Remember my previous job, where the goalposts always moved? When I started my own business, I found I was still doing that to myself! Every time I reached a goal, it was time to set the next, more challenging goal without rest or celebration.

People in this mindset often get stuck because instead of doing any Big Thinking, they stay in the safe zone of focusing on the small, easy routine, checking things off the to-do list so they feel like they've accomplished something and are *doing enough*. Influenced by the motivational triad, they avoid thinking about things that don't look easy or clear-cut — those don't bring instant gratification.

The worst thing about this limiting belief is that it also keeps people from prioritizing their relationships and their own emotional health.

One of my clients, Dominique, is a dietician dealing with patients who have a specific type of disorder. She believed that if she wasn't constantly available to her clients, they would disappear. This limiting belief prevented her from doing what she really wanted to do — take Tuesdays off to be with her three-year-old son.

Her assumption about her clients turned out to be untrue. Today, she happily enjoys her time with her toddler on Tuesdays, and her business continues to thrive.

Hyper-achievers have a hard time getting off the hamster wheel. Unfortunately, an illness or physical setback sometimes forces them to slow down.

But this doesn't have to happen to you. With self-awareness and perhaps the help of a coach, you can learn to take a second to pause and tap into the better parts of your judgment. Learn to celebrate your achievements and realize how much you're really doing. The results may surprise you. Often, hyper-achievers actually accomplish more when they're not so focused on achievement.

Liberating Truth: "I am doing PLENTY, and it's celebration-worthy!"

Limiting Belief #4: "There Isn't Enough" (Scarcity)

I often say to my clients, "Scarcity is a lie."

When we began our work, Dominique told me there just weren't enough patients affected by the disorder she specializes in who would pay for her services. The problem with that story is that it doesn't jibe with the facts. Statistics show there are lots of families that need her services. Her successful business now proves it. But just think what would have happened if she had continued believing her false assumption.

This scarcity idea often comes up around resources like money — "I don't have enough money to invest $40K in my business. What if I don't make it back?" Another resource is time. You might think there isn't enough time for you to make a big change in your life. ("I'm too old to be scaling a business.") Or you don't have time to pursue your goals. Maybe you're telling yourself, "I'm a great mom, so I don't want to push it and try to have a great business," — as if there's only so much success to go around, and you've had your share. But that's just silly.

People in this mindset often don't recognize it's a limiting belief. They think it's a fact. They have to change their mindset to re-write their story. Learn to recognize fact from fiction — it will change your life.

Liberating Truth: "There is PLENTY of what I need, and not only will I find it, I'll make the most of it."

LEARN TO
RECOGNIZE
FACT FROM
FICTION — IT
WILL CHANGE
YOUR LIFE.

Limiting Belief #5: "I'm Not Ready" (Fear of Success)

We've already talked about the fear of success, but now let's talk about the resulting belief — "I'm not ready." It's one of the most common limiting beliefs.

What it really means is, "I'm not ready for change." Because success does bring change — and change, even from something good, can take us out of our comfort zone into the unknown. Anything can happen! Enter worst-case-scenario thinking.

This limiting belief leads to a strange situation in which you may constantly sabotage your own results, yet you don't realize that's what you're doing. You may not even understand an underlying assumption is hampering you. You just keep trying... but you don't get anywhere.

One good way to deal with worst-case-scenario thinking is to ask yourself how you perceive success. Does it mean you'll no longer have time for your family? You'll have so much work you'll burn out? You'll have to spend too much time doing something you don't love? Address your underlying negative assumptions so they no longer have hidden power. You can control the scenario — it doesn't have to end up as the worst-case scenario.

Because guess what? You ARE ready. You're always ready. What is the worst thing that could happen? Is it worse than where you are right now? Most likely, no. So, let's go! Just do it!

Liberating Truth: "I'm ready RIGHT NOW."

Do You Need Counseling or Therapy?

Many limiting beliefs come from emotions related to past trauma. If you have problems dealing with issues from your past, you may benefit from counseling or therapy. In fact, my clients often ask about the differences between counseling/therapy versus coaching.

Here's the difference: Counselors and therapists are there to help you understand how past hidden traumas and other beliefs are affecting your emotional health. Their job is to help you be OK in the present. But they aren't there to give you suggestions as to what to do moving into the future.

Coaches, on the other hand, take you from the present into the future. We help you make decisions about what's next and navigate as you forge your path ahead. We're there when the going gets rough, and you want to turn back. We're there to support and guide you to continue to move toward your dream or goal or to make your desire a reality. We're your partner when you want to turn the impossible into the possible and then make it inevitable.

Coaching will only have limited benefit if past issues are hampering you. Often, a client can benefit by doing counseling and coaching simultaneously or by working with a therapist or counselor and then returning to coaching. The main goal is to make sure you're in the best mental space for you to succeed at achieving your dreams — whatever it takes.

YOUR GPS IS NOW SATELLITE-READY

I hope you've identified at least some of the limiting beliefs that have kept you stuck. If not, I strongly suggest you work with a coach to help.

If you have realized what's holding you back, now the real fun begins.

With your Snapshot of your Seven Life Facets that you put together in the previous chapter, you know the facts of your situation. With the understanding of the limiting beliefs that have kept you stuck, you've now identified and untangled all your conflicting instructions to your mental GPS. It is now cleared and ready for you to plug in your destination and plot your route to Point B — and beyond. You're on a journey, and Point B is just the first stop on the long, exciting road ahead.

As with any journey, you're probably thinking about whether you should pack more snacks or make a quick phone call before you hit the road. Or maybe this isn't the best day to do this; after all, there's a chance of bad weather.

But you're Thinking Big, and you've already made your Extraordinary Commitment. So now, you don't have any excuses. And do you really want excuses? Because I think you're ready. And you have what it takes — I know you do because you're reading this book!

It's time to plan your next adventure.

PRIORITIZE TO CREATE MARGIN

In your Snapshot, where you assessed your Seven Life Facets, you identified the things with the biggest stakes that could move the needle the most if you fixed them. Though you may have the urge to jump in and start knocking those out, I want you to hold off for now.

Instead, your first job is to give yourself a Strategic Pause — to make time and allow mental space for the planning activities in the next chapters. This is your opening for Thinking Big and the runway to creating your Big Plan. You'll need to give yourself permission to leave some of the facets alone for a while.

To create your Strategic Pause, consider what tasks, projects, or changes would create the biggest margin and give you the space in your schedule and your mind to Think Big. You may already have some on your Seven Facets list, but you may need to add new ones. For instance, even if one of your facets is going well, maybe hiring someone within that facet would create more time for you. That hire could be a priority for creating your Strategic Pause.

Once you have your tasks/projects/changes that will create that needed margin and opportunity for a Strategic Pause, how do you decide what to do first?

This is a perfect time to use one of my favorite tools: the Eisenhower Matrix.

URGENT VS. IMPORTANT: THE EISENHOWER MATRIX

President Dwight Eisenhower developed the concept of the Eisenhower Matrix.[10] He used it throughout his career to help him make decisions.

The matrix allows you to identify what is urgent and what's not urgent, what is important and what's not important (see Fig. 6.1). You can use it to plot anything you need to do, but we're going to use it to plot the tasks, projects, or changes you just decided you'll need to give yourself margin for the larger planning exercises we're about to do.

Though we're focusing on giving yourself margin in the short term for planning, the Eisenhower Matrix, in general, is a tool that can help you decide what you're going to do today, tomorrow, this week, this month, this quarter, and maybe even this year — because it allows you to sort your priorities out in advance. So you'll be using it later, too.

Figure 6.1 The Eisenhower Matrix

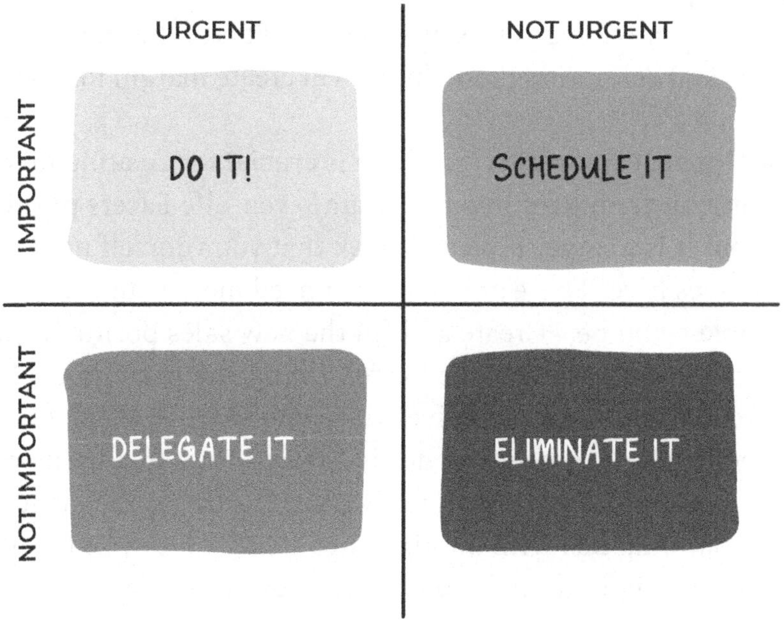

	URGENT	NOT URGENT
IMPORTANT	DO IT!	SCHEDULE IT
NOT IMPORTANT	DELEGATE IT	ELIMINATE IT

1. Plot the Tasks

Urgent/Important: Put items that need to be done ASAP to create margin here. These are things you'll do right away — today or tomorrow — and they aren't that difficult to tackle. A margin-creating example could be, "Set an hour of focus time on my calendar for each morning." I like to think of the Urgent/Important box as a place for tasks.

Urgent/Not Important: If an item needs to be done ASAP due to the demands of others but doing it doesn't create margin for you, and/or you don't have to be the one doing it, put it in Urgent/Not Important. Think of this as meaning it's urgent but not important for *you yourself* to do it. An example could be "Pay taxes" if they're due in the next couple of days. You can delegate most of the task to your spouse or your accountant except for providing your signature, etc. This is the "delegate" box — and delegating these things will create margin for you.

Not Urgent/Important: If an item is crucial for creating margin or long-term gain in one of your Seven Life Facets priorities, but it is a larger project or task that you yourself need to do, it goes here. These are items that need more planning. An example could be, "Create and fill the new sales position." In this case, while it may take longer, filling the position could create margin for you if it gives you someone to delegate to or someone who can help you do things and thus free up more of your time within the next few weeks. (As this is the longer-term planning box with multiple-step items, and we're focusing on the short term for our margin exercise, you may not have anything to put in this box right now.)

Not Urgent/Not Important: If an item doesn't create as much margin as other items and it isn't urgent or important, it goes here. During this current exercise for creating margin, you would probably only use this box if you're trying to decide what to delegate right now versus what can be postponed so you're not overloading others with delegated tasks all at once.

2. Determine Your Top Three Margin-Creating Areas

Look at all the items in your Urgent/Important box and decide on the **three most important things** that will provide the most margin for more planning as you revamp your business goals and main priorities over the next few weeks. (We'll cover that planning process in the next few chapters.)

Here's an example. Susan has put several margin-creating things in the Urgent/Important box related to her mental health and her relationships. She's concerned about her mental health because she's been having panic attacks. She has also been having relationship issues with her husband and one of her daughters, which is creating even more stress.

She has made the following list of margin-creating items:

- Block out an uninterrupted half hour each morning to plan the day. (This will create margin in her schedule.)
- Block out two hours each Friday afternoon that will be off-limits to any meetings, intrusions, or other concerns, so I can review weekly goals and do deep planning. (This will also create margin in her schedule.)

- Make family counseling appointment. (This will help her relieve some tension with her daughter so she has more emotional margin.)
- Make a doctor appointment to address panic attacks. (This will help her get her mental health in order.)
- Talk to husband about starting weekly date nights. (This will help relieve stress at home, freeing up more mental energy.)
- Buy a book on meditation. (This will help her deal with her panic attacks so she can focus better at work.)

Thinking a little more deeply, she realizes having more time to plan will actually help resolve her panic attacks because she'll have time to ground herself and feel more in control of her business. Therefore, in Urgent/Important, she chooses to prioritize the two scheduling tasks plus the family counseling, feeling that this combination will help the most.

As for the rest of her margin-creating activities, she may do any of them soon, too, but these top three take precedence over everything else in the Urgent/Important box. She knows that once she does those three tasks, the rest will be easier.

Then, looking at the Urgent/Not Important box, she realizes there are two quick-turnaround projects she can delegate to her assistant director to give herself even more planning time. Also in that section, she realizes she can add "Pick up kids from school every day" as an item to delegate since it isn't "important" for her to do personally. She decides to ask her husband to split this with her, and if he can't, then she'll hire a babysitter to pick the kids up and take care of them three evenings a week so she can stay later at work to finish important items. These solutions, combined with the others from the Urgent/Important box, will create even more margin for her. She doesn't put anything in the Not Urgent/Important box yet, as those things will take longer to complete and won't add margin right away. Those go in the "No for now" Not Urgent/Not Important box.

3. Address the Items You've Listed in Each Box

Here's how:

- DO the things in your Urgent/Important box. The sooner, the better. Schedule them ASAP in your calendar for today or tomorrow.
- Delegate the things in your Urgent/Not Important box.
- If you have any items in the Not Urgent/Important box, break those into smaller chunks and schedule them incrementally.
- Eliminate (or at least postpone) the things in your Not Urgent/Not Important box. You don't have to completely eliminate them; just consider them "parked" for now, and give yourself permission not to worry about them.

Keep in mind that this exercise is time-related. We're talking about RIGHT NOW. When everything feels important, what needs to be most important right now? When it's been resolved, something else can move into the Right Now slot. You'll get to everything you need to — just not all at once.

ADOPT A MINDSET OF
EXTRAORDINARY ACHIEVEMENT

This prioritization process to create margin for Big Planning is vital for you as an entrepreneur.

You're already extraordinary, but you've been getting in your own way. We've just addressed that problem.

Our goal now is to get you working in your Zone of Extraordinary Achievement, in which you create more energy — not just for you, but for everyone else you're working with or for. This is part of your value to everyone around you as an entrepreneur.

When you're working in your Zone of Extraordinary Achievement:

- You bring new products and services to your clients.
- You bring new opportunities to your team.
- You bring incredible potential to your relationships with family and friends.
- New worlds open because you create them.

And if you're doing it right, it comes naturally. Yes, it's hard work, but it's rewarding — and it's the work only *you* can do — in your unique way.

When you think about it like that, you not only cannot afford to stay stuck in your Parking Lot, you owe it to everyone else to get unstuck as soon as you can.

What would be possible if you went from being parked in a car with major mechanical issues to cruising comfortably down the highway in a fuel-efficient car you loved toward an amazing destination? You're operating

YOU NOT ONLY CANNOT AFFORD TO STAY STUCK IN YOUR PARKING LOT, YOU *OWE IT* TO EVERYONE ELSE TO GET *UNSTUCK* AS SOON AS YOU CAN.

on all cylinders, engine purring, and the car handles like a dream.

In that vehicle, the impossible becomes inevitable.

It's time to get a new vehicle that can take you where you want to go. That's coming in the next chapter — so make sure to give yourself the time and permission to make whatever changes you need. You need time to build your new custom vehicle and set it up just the way you want — because you're going to some amazing places, and you're going to take a lot of great people there with you.

THINK BIGGER: START LIBERATING YOURSELF

1. Identify three limiting beliefs and shift them into liberating truths. (This can be hard. Message me on one of my social media accounts listed on the About the Author page if you need help.)

2. What projects or tasks did you put into the Urgent/Important box in the Eisenhower Matrix? How will they give you margin to do your Big Planning?

3. What projects or tasks are in the Not Important boxes? And why?

4. How would it feel to delegate or eliminate any of the projects in the Not Important boxes? If you have tried to delegate in the past and it didn't work, why? Do you notice any fears or limiting beliefs around delegating?

If you're still having trouble making these decisions, you may want to think about working with a coach who can help you figure out what's going on.

BIG VISION: PAINT YOUR NEW BIG PICTURE

WHAT DOES 100 PERCENT LOOK LIKE?

*H*ere's a simple question: What if you operated at 100 percent of your capacity?

Imagine what you could do.

You'd be extraordinarily committed, fearless, and able to meet any challenge head-on.

In short, you would be amazing.

When I work with my clients, I take them through a detailed planning process that helps them figure out exactly what they need to succeed.

That process would probably fill an entire book on its own, so I can't give you the whole thing here. However, I can give you the main pieces you need to create a viable plan for yourself. These include a set of Vision Components and a set of Action Components. We'll be looking at the Vision Components in this chapter.

The Vision Components include:

- **A power sentence:** A statement about yourself that fuels your vision.
- **A 10-year vision:** A picture of where you want to be in 10 years.
- **A Belief Plan:** Direction from Future You to get where you want to go.
- **Your three-year target:** A map for the major strategies over the next three years that will move you closer to the 10-year vision.

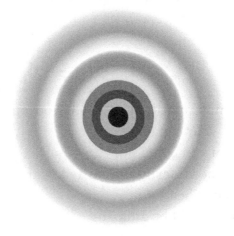

The further out you are from your Big Picture, the fuzzier it gets — and that's OK. Your 10-year vision doesn't have to be as clear as your three-year target, which in turn won't be as crystal-clear as the shorter-term components you'll be planning in the next chapter.

WHO ARE YOU? CRAFT YOUR POWER SENTENCE

It's time to craft your one magical sentence. To do that, we're going to step into the future for a moment and have a word with someone you need to know: Future You.

She is 10 years ahead of Present You, and during those 10 years, she was Thinking Big and accomplished all that she set out to do. She knows a lot about where you're going because she's been there. We're going to ask her to tell us who you really are under all those doubts, fears, and limiting beliefs. What are you really made of, and what's your true potential?

So call her into your mind and ask her now.

"Who am I, really? What am I capable of?"

Now, write down her answer. What does she know about you that you don't? You're going to use that information to create your power sentence. Whatever she tells you, write down — even if you can't believe it. You don't get to judge. You just need to write.

Next, you're going to take what she said and put it into a single sentence. This sentence should be in present tense, and it should be written from a first-person perspective.

You're writing it about yourself, so it should start with, "I am."

- "I am a brilliant leader running a thriving company with a talented team that loves providing a valuable service to hundreds of clients each year."
- "I am a confident, healthy business owner and great mom, and I know how to solve problems so creatively that I never have to sacrifice anything to get exactly what I want."
- "I am a skilled practitioner with a seven-figure business that I built from the ground up, and my excellent reputation makes me a sought-after keynote speaker and consultant in my field."

What does Future You say about you?

The next step along the path is being your future self now. If you visualize yourself every day the way Future You describes you, it's almost impossible not to make that future happen. Living as if you already are your Future You gives you confidence and fuel to create that future. And the how becomes easy. Your identity can change in an instant. It's just another decision you can make. Thinking, "That only happens to other people," or "That's just a dream that will never come true," is just accepting another limiting belief.

Keep that in mind as we continue our time-traveling journey.

YOUR 10-YEAR VISION:
100 PERCENT AND ALL-IN

Now it's time to pan out and look at the Big Picture in 10 years. We're going to study that through the lens of a question that will require you to Think Big.

What is your vision for 10 years from now if you were using 100 percent of your capacity?

Where would you be a decade from now? What would your business look like? Where do you want to be?

These answers give you a 10-year vision.

What is your dream?

All right: I get it. Even after all the work we've done, you might still be hesitating. "I have a dream, but I don't even want to say it because I feel like it's impossible," you say.

Good! That's exactly what you should feel.

In their book, *Built to Last,* Jim Collins and Jerry I. Porras introduced the concept of BHAGs — Big, Hairy, Audacious Goals. The two defined these goals as "having a long-term vision so daring in scope as to seem impossible."[11]

Your best future cannot come into being if you won't even take the crucial step of allowing it to form in your imagination.

A 10-year vision puts you in the mode of taking leaps versus baby steps. When you have a 10-year vision, you give yourself the opportunity to focus on the future, make decisions based on that future, and shift your thinking from "What am I doing today that impacts today?" to "What am I doing today that fuels tomorrow?"

This is truly what it means to focus on the ends rather than the means. The end is the 10-year vision, a bigger-than-life picture of what you want to accomplish and where you want to be.

BE CREATIVE AND HAVE FUN WITH IT

A lot of us are familiar with doing "vision and purpose" work, whether in a leadership development course, reading a book, or listening to a podcast. However, knowing how to do it doesn't make it simple, especially when our thoughts and feelings get in the way.

Arianna felt stressed out and spread too thin — stuck between the desire to grow her business and the challenge of trying to do it all at once. Even just thinking about creating one-year goals (and working toward them) in her business stressed her out. She was busy just trying to keep up with her workload and life demands.

So when I mentioned creating a 10-year vision, her eyes glazed over. That just seemed impossible.

"I can't even figure out what I want to do this week," she said.

But she needed to be more intentional with the decisions she was making to get back more time. We, therefore, needed to figure out where she was going. Where was her GPS taking her? If she circled the same parking lot or roundabout over and over, nothing would really change.

"You don't have to think of it as a photograph," I told her. "Think of it more as creating a painting on the wall, with fuzzy lines and tonal colors. More of a Renaissance painting than modern art."

She immediately perked up. This mental painting would serve as the 10-year vision. It was a picture of where she was heading.

Now it seemed a lot more doable — even fun.

So, we painted the vision — a revenue of $2M, five associates, and one administrative assistant, with Arianna handling five major campaigns a year and associates handling

40-60 more, possibly even adding video into the mix as well. With that, we could create a concrete business plan with actionable steps and a long-term roadmap.

The process surprised Arianna. We'd barely broken a sweat, and now we had valuable, actionable new information.

"Your brain will come up with the answers as long as you have the dream," she said.

THE BELIEF PLAN

I first heard about Belief Plans from Stacy Boehman.[12]

A Belief Plan is a set of beliefs that will inspire you to take action in order to create the results you seek. You already created one of these with your power sentence.

These beliefs are based on the identity of a person who has already achieved the outcome. The idea is to step into that identity and become it in your belief so you can be it in practice.

Create Your Belief Plan

Create a simple belief plan following these steps.

1. **Write your answers to these questions on a piece of paper:**

   - What thoughts can you hold right now that will fuel your inspiration, excitement, motivation, and certainty? "I am a prolific artist, and people pay top dollar for my work." "No one else knows how to do design quite like I do, and hundreds of people need my services."

"I love sales because I enjoy helping my customers."
"I am the Chosen One; I was born to do this."

- What will increase your confidence in moving toward your goal? "This is a great learning opportunity." "I love experimenting with new ideas." "I know exactly how to do this." "I have a great support network that will help me to achieve this quickly." "I am destined to solve this problem."

2. **Post the paper in a place where you can look at it every day.** Your mind's goal for the day is to believe these thoughts. It is simple.

3. **Decide on a measurable result to prove you believe those thoughts.** For example, "I'll know I am an outstanding salesperson because I'll pitch the big offer and get a YES!" "I'll know I am a prolific artist who gets top dollar because I'll sell two unique works this week."

Make it your job this week to try on these beliefs like a new outfit and wear them all day. It might be uncomfortable at first, but after a while, you'll get used to them and start to believe them, and great things will happen.

THE THREE-YEAR TARGET

So you know who you are, what you are, and where you're going. Now it's time to sharpen your colored pencils and get a little more specific in designing a strategic plan.

We're limiting it to three years, not 10, because any longer isn't practical. According to Gino Wickman[13] in his book *Traction*, "With life and business moving as fast as it does in the 21st century, there is little value in detailed strategic planning beyond a three-year window. A lot can change during that time span."

Three years is great because it takes you toward your vision, but at the end of the three years, you can reexamine your vision and create a new strategic plan for your current situation.

This three-year target will do two things:

- It allows those around you to *see* what you're saying and determine if and how they could be part of the scenario. It helps them see your vision.
- It improves your one-year planning process. You can determine the next best step to keep you on track over the next year much more easily when you have a clear three-year target.

A three-year target is simple but powerful. It includes measurables and a fleshed-out scenario.

You're still painting a picture of the destination, and it's coming more into focus, but you're not discussing every obstacle along the way.

The Three-Year Target Process

Think of your three-year target as a strategic plan. To create your own, follow these steps:

1. Determine your revenue, profit, and measurables (what are you going to track?) for the business three years from now.

2. Make a bulleted list of what the business will look like in three years, using descriptive language.

3. Make a bulleted list of what YOU will look like — mentally, physically, emotionally — in three years, using descriptive language.

4. Read through your three-year target every morning as part of your daily routine.

5. Review the business-side objectives with your team at least once a quarter.

6. Review all your objectives with a coach or an accountability partner at least once a quarter.

A Three-Year Target in Action

When Arianna and I set out to develop her three-year target, her loudest (even though he was behind the scenes) and most important team member at the time was her husband. He needed to get on board with her desire and drive to make it happen.

- Arianna determined she would create a revenue of $350K and profit of 35 percent.
- She would start a payroll, so she would be paying herself within the confines of the business.

- She would measure the number of leads, conversions, initial sale amount, final sale amount, and time spent on marketing.
- Her business would be comprised of two associates and an administrative assistant.
- She would shoot eight campaigns over a four-month timeframe, her associates would shoot sixteen more, and the assistant would handle some social media and other duties for Arianna's business, giving Arianna more time for leadership and management responsibilities.

Her husband needed to be on board with her Big Thinking and desire for an extraordinary life for some of her guilt to dissipate. Had she ever asked him what he desired? What kind of life he wanted? No, she hadn't. So that was step one.

Ironically, she found that he wanted the same. She had wasted all that energy and time in fear for no reason.

Next, I encouraged her to show him the numbers because they really did tell a picture. And the numbers meant mapping out the time she planned to spend at work (and that included editing time in her home office) and time at play. So she literally printed out an old-school calendar and wrote in her time plan. That's part of the numbers.

Once her husband saw the revenue potential alongside the planned work hours, as well as what Arianna desired, his attitude shifted. He truly became a part of the team in her eyes. His support made her decisions as a mom, spouse, and business owner much easier.

Arianna was now all set, with a newly programmed destination in her GPS, a rebuilt vehicle, a supportive co-traveler, and a fuel tank that was topped off. She was ready to roll.

WHY DO I NEED A 10-YEAR VISION IF MY TARGET IS ONLY THREE YEARS OUT?

We distinguish goals using three lengths: short-term, medium-term, and long-term. Short-term goals are those you can accomplish from right now to a year from now. Medium-term goals may take from two to five years. Long-term goals may take up to 10 years.

These goals fold into each other. We work backward from the 10-year vision, so we know where we're going. But the farther away the vision is, the fuzzier things get, which makes it a good idea to have a target that is closer — at three years. But without detailed steps along the way, we can't measure our progress or see if we're on track, which leads us to our one-year goals and plan (which we'll talk about in the next chapter).

A 10-year timeframe for business planning is longer than most forecasting and is subject to more changes. But because many businesses, including your competitors, are unlikely to have thought that far ahead, a 10-year business vision can help you stay a step ahead in the marketplace.

When you have these components, you can examine your Seven Life Facets and pull out your Eisenhower Matrix periodically to assess your priorities. Are they moving you toward your target? Are they part of your three-year target? Is anything missing?

When you do these exercises, your priorities can shift — sometimes even drastically. I've already told you about Lindsey's journey from chaos to order and calm. At the beginning, all her tasks were in the Urgent/Important box. She had nothing — no Snapshot or Big Plan — to measure their importance with. Until she looked at her data, she was just guessing about what was important. Once she could clearly see what to do, plan, delegate, and eliminate, her life started to sort itself out.

And there is no doubt about it; a 10-year vision is larger than life. It's definitely Thinking Big.

Now that these components are clear, let's move into the details — your one-year goals. We'll start setting these, along with creating some ways to manage them, in the next chapter.

THINK BIGGER: YOUR BIG PICTURE

1. Who is the Future You? What does she think and feel? How is she different from Present You?

2. What limiting beliefs sprang to mind as you created your power sentence, 10-year vision, and three-year target? Push yourself to shift them into more empowering thoughts.

3. What can you do to step more fully into your power sentence? How can you use it to fuel your motivation each day? Pick one way to use your power sentence and start doing it right away. Not tomorrow — today.

4. What does it look and feel like to be "all-in"? Does having an "all-in" mindset scare you or excite you? Why?

CHAPTER 8

BIG ACTIONS: TAKE CHARGE OF YOUR LIFE

Create the highest, grandest vision possible for your life because you become what you believe.

— Oprah Winfrey

BIG ACTION COMPONENTS

To create the next phase of your Big Plan, we'll need to drill down further and create the following:

- Your one-year goals
- Your quarterly focus areas
- Your support systems

WHY ONE-YEAR GOALS MATTER

Remember in high school when there were the jocks, the nerds, the theater geeks, and the courtyard people?

Well, enter a new category: The anti-goal crowd.

Sometimes I get on a consult call, and I hear women say things like:

- "I don't love goals."
- "I don't set goals."
- "I never reach them, so why set them?"

The good news is that when they learn to shift their thinking to the Big Plan:

- They figure out that having goals is really the key to happiness.
- They become confident not just in setting goals but in achieving them.

If you're someone who cringes at the word goals, you probably fall into one of three camps:

1. Women who don't have goals.
2. Women who have goals but aren't writing them down.
3. Women who have goals written down but aren't achieving them.

If you're reading this book, you probably fall into the second or third category.

If you're in the second, you're probably interested in having goals, but you haven't committed to them (like we discussed in Chapter 4). You're interested in reducing your stress, being more productive, finding more time in your day, making more money, and hiring a team. You've taken some small steps to get the support you need to do this — like reading this book —but you haven't taken any leaps. You haven't committed to achieving these goals.

If you're in the third category of women, you're used to setting goals, BUT not the kind of goals that will really and truly move the needle in your business or at home. You may have goals for accomplishing things today, but they are things you always accomplish, not a target farther out in the future that requires you to change what you're doing.

But here's the hard truth: Setting goals is what leads to achievement. Here's an example.

Having No Goals: Life Is Just a Dream

For the last year, you've dreamed of moving your business into a new office. Instead of working at home from your kitchen table, you'll have your own professional location with space to add some team members as you grow your business. You've thought of the perfect client experience — a bright, airy reception area with a friendly receptionist (versus hearing kids crying in the background when you're on a call) who will make your clients comfortable and offer them coffee. When you're ready to meet with them, you'll welcome them into the big, sunlit conference room, where you can present your ideas using the latest technology that lets them know you're a pro in your field. When they leave, they're already convinced to give you their business.

Unfortunately, you haven't been able to figure out how to fund this dream. You don't have much of a budget, and you aren't able to pay yourself consistently, let alone fund a whole new building! Plus, you're constantly wondering if you have enough saved up for emergencies or once-a-year subscriptions and expenses as it is. Your dream of an office is just that — a dream. It's a fantasy that gets you through the tough days, but you've never truly entertained it as a potential reality.

... Vs. Setting Clear Goals: Life Is an Adventure

For the last year, you've dreamed of moving your business into a new office. Instead of working at home from your kitchen table, you'll have your own professional location with space to add some team members as you grow your company. And in fact, you haven't been just dreaming — you've been planning, too. You're determined to transform the dream into a reality. Your business has grown to the extent that you can't wait anymore — it's time to take it to the next level so you can start wowing higher-end clients.

You've done your research, and you know exactly what you need and how much it will cost. It will take a large financial investment, so you look at your budget, where you track all your spending and earnings consistently. You know your projected revenue for the next several months and your current average monthly expenses, so you can determine where to allocate funds to start saving for the down payment. You decide to set a goal of $30K for initial design and furniture expenses, which you'll achieve by the end of this year. You have also forecasted your monthly rental and utilities budget in preparation for the new costs. And finally, you project that within the next two years, you'll be hiring an assistant, so you'll need some extra space for that person so you won't have to move again right away. By your projections, the ROI in higher sales due to increased exposure at the high-traffic locations you've researched should easily offset the investment.

You've ensured you can keep paying yourself a consistent amount each month, so you won't need to sacrifice any personal income. You see some places where you can shave off business expenses to achieve the goal on time. And you already set money aside each month for unexpected miscellaneous items, so you can dip into some of that, too. Breaking your $30K goal into quarterly, monthly, and weekly increments, you set your finance app to start allocating the money you'll need each week, adjusting for lower-revenue seasons. Now you have a clear plan, and all you have to do is follow it each week. It all works out, and by next December, you're meeting with a real estate agent to start looking for the perfect space to rent.

Which situation sounds better?

SET YOUR ONE-YEAR GOALS

To set goals that get you somewhere, two things need to happen:

1. You need to change your thinking around what goal setting is all about.
2. The goals you set need to be SMARTER.

Flip the Script: Priorities vs. Goals

What if you thought about your list of goals as a list of priorities that you act on? Here's why thinking about them as priorities changes everything:

1. **You can't fail on a list of priorities.** You cannot fear not reaching the priority (like you might be scared of feeling like a failure for not reaching the goal). You can't *achieve* a priority; you're just working within it as an area of focus, though you may be doing specific items to develop that area of priority. (Remember: You're either winning or learning.)

2. **You don't feel a need to wait for the right time with a list of priorities.** Often, we delay tackling a goal until the timing is right. But timing is built into the word priorities. The *Cambridge Dictionary* defines a priority as "something that is very important and must be dealt with before other things."[14] When you have priorities, you don't wait for life to happen to you; you take control of life and make things happen.

3. **You create your own list of priorities using your own agency.** You choose. You decide what is important.

4. **You take your constraints into account when establishing your priorities.** Given the amount of time, money, people/relationships, or brain power you have (your constraints), you choose what is a priority and what is not.

If you think your schedule is too full, that really tells you what your priority should be: cleaning up how you're using your time!

5. **You can't get stuck on the *how* before you accept a list of priorities.** It's a priority, so figuring out the how is assumed.

6. **You can't get trapped in the idea you have to love your priorities.** Clients often get stuck because they think they need to *love* a goal. That makes a goal sort of like a boss — something external that you're working *for*. When it's hard work, and you're in a tough situation, if you think the goal is in charge, it's easier to abandon it — to quit working for it as your boss. But with priorities, suddenly the pressure is off to *love* them — instead, you *have* them, and you *work from* them — they're part of you and your vision. They may excite you and feel a little risky, but they're also part of your own desire. They're in you, not outside you.

7. **You're the only one in charge of your priorities.** I hear many women say, "What will other people think of these goals, especially if I don't meet them?" Changing your thinking from goals to priorities helps tone down the stress of *other people* because only you can determine your priorities. You don't even need to share a list of priorities if you don't want to.

8. **Your priorities are continuous focus areas, and they aren't right or wrong.** Were you worried that you

didn't have the *right* goal? (Maybe there's another potential goal out there languishing, and you've missed
it!) A priority is just something that is important to
you at the time. It's a decision you've made. Someone
else may have a different opinion about what is important — but that's fine. They get to have their priorities, too. They don't have to be yours, and vice versa.

It doesn't matter what you call them as long as
they motivate you to move forward and provide a constant reminder of what you want to achieve.

Set SMARTER Goals

One of the most well-known goal-setting techniques is
SMART. The acronym encourages us to make goals specific,
measurable, agreed-upon (some people use achievable or at-
tainable), realistic, and time-bound.

Over time, different people have used different words to
specify what each of the letters stands for, and some have
expanded the acronym, too.

Michael Hyatt's "SMARTER goals" framework is the one
I use when I am working with my clients.[15]

Here's the acronym I use, as adapted from Hyatt:

Specific: When your goal is targeted toward something specific, it's more motivating. You know exactly what you're trying
to accomplish. Vague goals create too much confusion, which
zaps your energy as you try to figure out the parameters.

Measurable: You must have some sort of way to measure
your progress or whether you've met the goal. Can you break

it into smaller chunks so you can see how far along you are? Could you put a numbers marker on it? "I'll sign 10 new clients by mid-year." "I'll have one date night a week with my spouse." "We'll increase net profits by 30 percent this year." "I'll go on five outings each quarter with my kids."

Actionable: What are the actions you'll take to achieve the goal? Determining actions can help you realize when you're setting unrealistic goals based on your desired timeframe. For instance, if you decide that to lose 30 pounds within your desired timeframe, you'll eat only 530 calories a day, that's not realistic (or healthy!). Because it's not actionable, it is doomed to fail, and that's demotivating. Actionable goals give you a clear, realistic picture showing exactly how your actions will achieve the result, which will help motivate you to stay on track.

Risky: Create goals that feel challenging and create new opportunities in ways that involve some risk. Pushing yourself out of your comfort zone will be much more rewarding and motivating than doing the status quo. Your goal should take you out of your Parking Lot and into an adventure.

Time-bound: The best goals create urgency, either through establishing deadlines or specific periodic checkpoints or milestones.

Exciting: This goes back to the need to involve your feelings. If you aren't excited about your goal, it will become one that lingers on your list, sucking away your energy till it falls off the list, never to be seen again. You'll abandon it at the first sign of difficulty. If it's exciting, you'll be much more likely to stick with it.

Relevant: Does this goal take you where you want to be? How does it relate to your values? Is it YOUR goal... or someone else's you feel you *should* do? Will it really move things forward for you, or is it a shiny object that will just distract you from what you need to do? Is it relevant in your current season of life? For example, the goal of living in Florida by yourself every winter is probably not relevant right now if you live in Minnesota and have school-age kids.

Example Goals

Here are a few examples of SMARTER goals:

- Gain three new clients each quarter by presenting at one high-level conference per quarter with ideal clients as attendees starting in Q2.
- Prepare marketing collateral and a specific website landing page three weeks prior to each event to track client traffic from these events to determine ROI.
- Create and launch a new service or product by the end of next quarter by preparing cost analysis, revenue projections, pricing structure, marketing plan, and budget.
- Gain five new clients in the next 90 days by holding one consult call each week.
- Starting June 1, spend two hours each week with each child alone doing an activity of their choosing.

How Many Goals/Priorities Should You Have?

When it comes to goals/priorities (I'll use these terms interchangeably), I believe you should have three to seven personal ones each year and three to seven for business. Beyond seven, we tend to lose focus. Each quarter, you should select one or two out of the bunch to work on; working on all goals always is unrealistic.

Do they have to go in the same document? No, they don't have to, but it's good to keep them together in a master document because our personal and business lives are intertwined. Remember the yarn.

Have copies of this one document everywhere. This is a living document; it's a document that you refer to regularly. No keeping it in the back of the drawer! Put a copy of your personal goals on your desk at home, or post them on your refrigerator so you see them every day. Keep a copy of your business goals in your project management system where everyone on your team can see them — and you can even track progress there to keep people motivated.

BREAKING IT DOWN FURTHER: YOUR QUARTERLY FOCUS AREAS AND TARGETED ACTIONS

Now that you have your vision for Future You, along with your one-year goals or priorities, it's time to focus and decide what actions you need to take NOW to achieve your vision. Just like my suggestion of three to seven goals, I suggest establishing three to seven areas of focus each quarter.

Some things to keep in mind: While these areas of focus feed or fuel your one-year goals, you don't have to feed each goal every quarter. There may be goals that aren't touched until quarter four, and that is OK.

Also, for the goals that are fed this quarter, it is important to set a due date. The last day of the quarter shouldn't be the due date for each area of focus. You'll fall into the trap of giving yourself too much time and procrastinating. Spread out your due dates. If others are collaborating with you, set the due dates with them. You can also delegate.

I take my clients through a detailed process for this aspect, which is too much for one book. However, one thing I do want to touch on is your Zone of Extraordinary Achievement — how to get everything working to your strengths, so you achieve maximum output.

WORK IN YOUR ZONE OF EXTRAORDINARY ACHIEVEMENT

The Zone of Extraordinary Achievement is vital to determine what goals you should prioritize and what you should delegate. It's based on some of Michael Hyatt's concepts related to the "Zone of Genius," which he outlines in *Free to Focus*.[16] His concepts guide people to do things they enjoy and are good at. These are in their Zone of Genius. However, my clients are entrepreneurs, so I use a system specifically tailored to their situations as business owners.

Entrepreneurs create. When they're on their game, they generate more for everyone. So as an entrepreneur, you're not only a power consumer; you're a *power generator*. We don't just look at what these focus areas do for you — we look at what they allow you to do for everyone. And looking beyond your

AS AN ENTREPRENEUR, YOU'RE NOT ONLY A *POWER CONSUMER*; YOU'RE A *POWER GENERATOR.*

business, this energy also goes to all your personal Life Facets — you'll bring more to your relationships, your health/wellness will benefit, your finances will straighten out, etc., and you'll have a better quality of life all around. The more you power up, the better you produce, and the more you bring to everyone around you — it's a win-win-win situation. When you're happy, everyone else has more opportunity to be happy, too.

If you have high energy input (enthusiasm, passion, drive) for a particular task, but you're not good at it, or it isn't a high-movement task, you're potentially putting in too much energy/time without a good ROI. Over time, this situation will reduce your achievement level.

The goal is to minimize these obstructions to get you to a level of Extraordinary Achievement — firing on all cylinders, making excellent decisions to maximize your strengths and minimize your weaknesses, and maintaining peak performance in all your Seven Life Facets.

Therefore, consider the following when you're deciding what to do yourself versus what to delegate or eliminate as you look at your goals:

1. **The amount of enthusiasm you have when you anticipate doing it — your *energy input*.** When you perform certain actions, you get more energy just from the excitement or enjoyment of doing them. These are things you would do whether someone paid you or not. These are your Power-Producing Actions. You just like doing them. Meanwhile, other actions are sheer torture — what Hyatt calls "drudgery." You hate doing them, whether you're good at it or not. These are Black Holes — they suck up time and effort, but you don't get anywhere except maybe behind.

2. **Whether or not the action can potentially create movement within your main priorities.** Sometimes, you might find yourself doing things you love, but they don't move any vital priorities forward enough to warrant the time spent on them. Keep in mind that some actions may seem at first like they're not moving anything forward, but that's because you're learning how to do them, and the skill you're building will pay off big later. So it's not necessarily a waste of your time as long as it's an area of learning that fits that description.

3. **If you're the only one who can do it.** If this is an action only you should do, and it's vital for that Life Facet, then you obviously can't delegate it. But if it's not something only you can do and there are other resources available to take it on, you'll need to think about whether it's better to delegate it versus doing it yourself.

4. **Whether or not you're good at the activity.** If you're putting a ton of enthusiasm and time into something that's important but is also a huge learning curve for you, it may not be worth continuing. You have to evaluate if there's a clear payoff. If it's something with high input but low output for you, consider taking it off your list and putting it on someone else's or just putting it on a list of "nice to have, but don't need to have" items for now.

   (For a great tool to look into your Zone of Extraordinary Achievement more deeply, check out the Think Big Toolkit available on my website at AndreaLiebross.com/toolkit.)

The Parked List: Your Idea Valet

One thing many entrepreneurs (especially super-creative ones) struggle with is ideas. The problem definitely isn't coming up with new ideas; they show up everywhere — while driving, while eating, and even while trying to work on other ideas.

The problem is managing them. You have to get them out of your head, or they'll just keep popping in like toddlers wanting attention.

Goals can be like that — and it's one way we get overcommitted. We have so many ideas about what we could do, but doing all of them is just not feasible.

Get them out of your head by writing them down. Keep an Idea Parking Lot. This is where you put your parked potential goals. They can stay there while you're working on another goal at the moment. This gives you peace of mind — you know they're there when you need them, and when you do, you can have the valet pull the right one up to the door. You don't have to go searching for it.

DESIGN YOUR SUPPORT SYSTEMS

First off, what do we mean by *systems*?

These can be as broad or as narrow as you choose to define them. But in my experience, systems are ways of doing things that support you in achieving your goals.

Most of them fall into three categories:

- Process Frameworks/Templates
- People/Culture, Delegation, Networking, and Professional Services
- Tools/Technology/Information and Automation

Systems are important because they support you in your goals. They create efficiency and make things easier — not just for you but for everyone else. They take away headaches and speed bumps. I like to follow the order above — process, people, tools — to address systems. Here's a way to think about it:

Examine your goals/priorities and where things are getting hung up. These are the pain points within the process. Here are some things to consider when you take a deeper look at why you aren't achieving your goals/priorities:

1. Does a process need to change? Address that first.

2. Are the people on your team (at home or in business!) on the same page as you (or each other)? Or is better communication needed?

3. Is everyone (especially you) working in their Zone of Extraordinary Achievement? If not, where can you shift tasks or delegate?

4. If things are all right with #1 and #2, but you need tools to make the work go more smoothly, what kind of tool will help? This is where you can get creative and look at your organization's culture (or if you're a solo entrepreneur, your own or your family's preferences).

You don't necessarily need the latest slick app or expensive smart board to solve a problem. There are companies that have a standup meeting around a wall where they use sticky notes to track their projects — and they prefer it this way because the wall is always there, visually reminding everyone to check it when they go past it to the bathroom or the kitchenette.

Systems are so specific to each situation that I could write an entire book on them alone. The main point is to be creative and have fun when you decide how to solve problems using systems. At the end of this chapter, I've listed some of my clients' systems for inspiration.

PROCESS FRAMEWORKS

You've already taken the first step toward shifting your processes for planning and goal/priority-setting. Once you have a plan for delegating things, you may have to redesign some or all of your internal processes for doing them because you'll need better communication and integration among the people now doing the tasks.

Again, you'll want to think these things through based on your specific situation. However, I've included one great process I want to share with you to get you started in managing your time effectively, and it works for any situation or person. It's available in the Think Big Toolkit at AndreaLiebross.com/toolkit.

PEOPLE NETWORKS

As support systems, these networks can be as broad or narrow as you like, but I suggest thinking broadly. Go beyond your work team or family and include medical and mental health professionals as well as other types of organizations such as your schools, church, and community centers. You should also consider professionals you can contract for specific jobs — anything from a marketing expert to a nanny or a coach! And don't forget family and friends. They can be invaluable allies.

When you know the kind of work you need to delegate, you'll have a better idea of where to start looking for the right people.

When you leverage others' skills and abilities, you give them opportunities to grow and develop, too. If you think about it that way, it's much more exciting than just thinking you're piling chores or tasks on them. If you ask them to do things that fall into their own Zones of Extraordinary Achievement (which won't be the same as yours), the tasks you see as Black Holes will excite them.

One more note: This may seem obvious, but I still need to mention it. When you add others to your support networks, make sure they're people you want to work with. Try to surround yourself with positive people who want to see you succeed. Avoid toxic people who will (either consciously or unconsciously) sabotage your efforts.

A Caution About Relationships

Entrepreneurs face their own special issues with relationships — especially with life partners. Their life partners need a certain level of understanding and acceptance, without which the entrepreneur faces added stress and potential failure. Entrepreneurs also face hidden threats when they seem to have good relationships. I have focused entire workshops and coaching sessions on this subject, and there are no easy answers. If you feel your relationship needs work or may be undermining your business, putting together your Big Plan may help crystallize things to make it better. But if not, get help. A coach can help you work through your own planning and crystallize your vision to make it clearer for your life partner.

SMART TOOLS

Tools and technology are great as long as you use them wisely. I'm putting these last because you shouldn't start planning tools or technology until you know who is doing what and how — in other words, your people and processes. Otherwise, you're planning your processes around your technology, which is backward thinking. Technology should always support the ideal process wherever possible, and sometimes technology isn't the answer — it adds more layers you don't need.

So, after you've designed your ideal general processes, ask questions that will help you leverage the support of technology in the best way possible. Whether it is an app, software, or a device, technology can support you in terms of connection, efficiency, ease, and flow.

1. **How can you leverage tools or technology to create connection?** Use video conferencing, email, social media, and other tools to connect where they will be most effective, but use caution — these can take up a lot of time with low ROI if not used strategically.

2. **How can you leverage tools or technology to make things more efficient and flow?** Workflow software, contact management, vacation planners, you name it! There's an app for that!

3. **Can you accomplish something more efficiently without technology?** Though it's less common in today's work from home culture, sometimes teams in the same physical location prefer to put up their workflow on a giant whiteboard or even sticky notes, so everyone can see it at any time, and it's always there as a reminder (versus hidden away on an electronic system somewhere). Your people, organizational culture, logistics, and other factors will influence which systems you use.

SYSTEMS IN ACTION

The right systems, big or small, can make life so much easier. For instance:

Arianna got support by hiring a nanny, using Instacart, bringing a photo editor and another photographer into her business, and taking a helper to every shoot.

Tamara got support by hiring her own personal assistant, enlisting a driver to pick her kids up from school, investing in software that tracks new leads, and bringing on a fractional CFO into her business.

Dominique got support by subscribing to a meal delivery service, hiring a dog walker, using a virtual assistant to post on social media, and using template software to develop all her forms and proposals.

My client Alex, who does speaking engagements, needed a system for following up on inquiries, booking gigs, and getting paid. She employed the Dubsado software system to organize, manage, and simplify all these tasks so she could focus on preparing for more opportunities and national exposure.

Brittany needed a better cash flow management system. She needed to know if she could afford to hire more employees. Her firm had outgrown its current spreadsheet system and QuickBooks, which only tells you after the fact what has already been spent. So she employed a new money management system.

Tamara was tired of being asked, "What's for dinner?" by her three boys every night. So she put up a chalkboard in the kitchen, and on Sundays, she filled it in with what was for dinner every night that week. No more asking and no more wondering!

What is your first support move?

THINK BIGGER: YOUR ACTION PLAN

1. When someone says goals, do you feel defeated or energized? Does the word "goals" work for you? Is the word "priorities" a better fit, and why?

2. Create your Belief Plan.

3. Create your one-year goals using the SMARTER format. Create your 90-day focus areas within your Zone of Extraordinary Achievement.

4. Look at last week. Did the way you used your time fuel your 90-day focus areas? What can you do differently this week to have better alignment?

5. Where do you need new or better systems? If you had them, what would be possible? Identify the next best step in creating new or better systems.

PART THREE

RESULTS

Navigate the Changes

CHAPTER 9

BIG FREEDOM: FUTURE YOU

The fruits of entrepreneurship are meaning and freedom.

— Maxime Lagacé

*C*laire came to me with many different concerns, but one, in particular, was anxiety over her finances. She had several credit cards on which she was carrying debt. She did not have her personal finances separated from her business finances. She wasn't looking at things systematically, which led to decisions she regretted or no decisions at all. Her lack of a real financial strategy impacted her whole mindset. She was constantly worrying about whether she had enough money — but that question was too vague to answer.

This fear dominated all her decisions. She only had one question she used as a filter for decisions: "Is this an opportunity for me to make money?" But the opportunities for her to make money weren't necessarily moving her in the direction she wanted to go, personally or professionally. Yes, she needed to make money, but she also wanted to live and do other things, especially travel.

To create a better system for her finances, Claire started using a software tool called You Need a Budget (YNAB) that helped her assign goals to her money. She now sits down every morning with her coffee and accesses her YNAB app to confirm what happened yesterday in all her bank accounts, make necessary adjustments, and plan her spending for the day and the future. This practice has led her to stop frantically saving and trying to bring in more money without any idea whether she needs to because now she not only knows she has plenty of money, but she also knows the easiest ways to make plenty more. And she knows exactly how having more money will help her achieve specific goals because she's allocated funds toward those goals. She has finally gained control of her thinking around money.

After a year of working together, she has made more money in her practice than any year before. She also figured out how to work and travel and vacation all at the same time. I never know what her Zoom background will be; she hops onto our coaching calls from all around the world. With that different way of looking at things, she was able to spend a month in France over the summer and two weeks in Caribbean in the fall. Due to a few simple changes in her approach and thinking, she's free of the shackles of anxiety that plagued all her other decisions and hampered her in so many other ways.

REAL FREEDOM: IT'S ALL IN YOUR MIND

Remember when you picked up this book? Maybe you felt like so many of the clients I've mentioned, like you've been working so hard yet not getting anywhere. One of the things they tell me as we begin working together is that no matter how hard they work, they can't get ahead. This feels burdensome. They want a sense of accomplishment — freedom from this burden.

The thing they invariably learn is that to have freedom, they have to think differently about their lives, which ultimately leads them to take different action.

Now that you've leveled up your mindset and put together a new plan (I hope) that embraces your goals and gives you time to accomplish them, you can see the problem wasn't that you needed to work harder; you needed to work differently.

Think about it like this. During all your hard work trying to make happen what you thought you were supposed to make happen, underneath, something else was trying to happen.

That something else was the next best version of you. And what you needed to do was to give her space. But instead, you were blocking her with your expectations, assumptions, and limiting beliefs.

Now that we've cleared all of those away, she can become who she needs to be.

This is what true freedom feels like.

And it all starts in your mind.

By going through this process, you've taken the steps to free yourself from the things that were holding you back. Here's a partial list:

- Guilt
- Old stories that no longer serve you
- Others' expectations
- Stuck Stress
- Financial anxiety

The sources of these things haven't gone away. Your reactions to them have merely changed.

BUILDING NEW TRAFFIC PATTERNS FOR YOUR BRAIN

As you've worked so hard to redirect your negative thoughts to more productive ones, you've actually rewired the neural pathways in your brain.

This is science. This isn't as "woo-woo" as some people make it sound. This is literally how the brain works.[17] (I knew there was a reason I loved neuroscience so much in college!)

When we start doing things a different way, our brains prune the synapses we aren't using anymore and strengthen the pathways for the activity we're doing more of — and that strength even carries over to similar activities. The more challenging and emotionally involved the activity, the better we'll remember it and engrain it for the future.

So as you get rid of thought patterns that aren't serving you and instead focus on new ones, eventually, you do become a new version of yourself.

We're all evolving all the time. It's just that most of the time, we do it unconsciously. We become slightly different versions of ourselves in various ways. In this case, we've consciously redirected the brain and created a new neural pathway that will give us a new, hopefully in the long run, automatic belief system that will generate useful emotions, which will help us be who we want to be in the world — like Claire, who wanted to own her own business and travel the world. Our new belief systems then lead us to useful actions that serve us and ultimately give us exactly what we're looking for.

REDEFINE FREEDOM

When you run your own business, you can create your own freedoms, and when you're free, you can live up to your potential. When you work for somebody else, you're not free to choose what you do, when you do it, and why you do it. Entrepreneurs often choose their path because they want what they consider freedom in four main categories: Time, money, relationships, and brain power — our four most valuable resources.

But these freedoms are more about how a person manages their mind than how they manage the resource itself. First, even the notion you have to be a business owner to have those freedoms isn't true. You can have them at any time. When I work with clients, they usually say they are seeking those kinds of freedoms, but I find the freedoms they believe they crave at the beginning of doing this work aren't the kinds they experience in the end.

As John Olivant wrote, wanting freedom is a universal human desire, but attaining it is the hard part because it is all in your thinking.[18] He explains that the way we define freedom regarding our resources affects how we think about them.

To examine our thinking, we need to realize there are two sets of ideas going on: Having more of a resource(s) versus having freedom in relation to the resources. Let's look in more depth at those concepts.

Freedom of Time

As a business owner and entrepreneur, you constantly juggle time constraints. You may have once fantasized about having freedom to do whatever you wanted with your time, but now, you may feel like that was an impossible dream.

However, that's all in your thinking. You can manage people who demand your time, and you can choose how much free time you have and what you do with it. If you think you should be available all the time to clients, staff, and family, that's not a problem with time but a problem with your thoughts about time.

Successful entrepreneurs manage time demands by managing their own minds. To manage your time, you have to free yourself from reacting to how you think you *should* be spending your time and start choosing where to spend your time. You choose your boundaries with time. Past You thought being available 24/7 created job security. Future You knows that's not true; those people will still be there when you're ready.

Freedom of Money

When I talk to my clients about money, most just tell me they want to make more. I ask, "How much more?" But they don't know. They don't even give themselves permission to establish a number. Setting a number is scary. What if they don't achieve it?

But is the real goal with money having piles of it or just not having to worry about it? Olivant says most people would choose the second option.

When my clients run their businesses well, they make money. How much depends on how they set prices, profit margins, and a number of other things. All those things are up to them. Think of Arianna, who made all her decisions about money with a specific goal in mind. She knows her market and how to appeal to them, and she is achieving her monetary goals. If you have what others want, and you know how to market yourself and run your business — if you know your own worth in dollars and sense — you'll make money.

Being free of worry about money is a whole different thing. It goes back to managing your mind. Anxiety over money doesn't stop just because you reach a certain amount or restrict your spending. *Believing* you have enough funds to do what you want, right here and now, without money being an obstacle, is the freedom.

Freedom of Relationship

Whom do you want to do business with? Who do you want on your team? You get to choose these people because you own your own business. Not only that, you get to choose *how you want to think about and interact with those people.* How to have a relationship is often far more important than whether to have it. We can learn and grow a great deal just by working through difficult situations with people.

By now, you know I am all about having the right people in the right seats. We think that "when we have the right people in place," everything will be a lot easier. But as your capacity to Think Bigger expands, you'll realize relationships with others are just a bunch of thoughts about how we interact with them and who we think they are. Those thoughts lead to feelings, which lead to actions, which lead to results. Sometimes you do need to let a team member go because they don't have the skills you need. But sometimes, before jumping to letting them go, consider whether you can help them learn things while you also gain skills in coaching performance better. This benefits both you and the other person.

We can have freedom in a relationship right now. We get to choose how we want to think about the angry client

HOW TO
HAVE A
RELATIONSHIP
IS OFTEN
FAR MORE
IMPORTANT
THAN
WHETHER TO
HAVE IT.

or the disgruntled team member. This goes for personal relationships, too. Exercising this freedom is important for your well-being. You want to spend more and more of your time surrounded just by people you click with, who you appreciate and who appreciate you, but realistically, you can't manage your life to include only those people. Freedom comes from changing your expectations around others' actions. Just as you love your kids though you don't always approve of their behavior, you can appreciate difficult people for what they do and deal with the issues without losing your peace of mind. Obviously, this doesn't mean tolerating abuse — but it does mean refusing to allow the behavior of another to control your own actions or thoughts. You get to choose how to respond emotionally and whether or not to be trapped in those emotions.

Even Positive Relationships Can Be Restricting

Women who inherit businesses often deal with the problem of trying to honor their family legacy while also finding their own way of doing things. Their loyalty to their parent(s) or the person from whom they inherited the business conflicts with the need to make their own decisions. This is an example of why managing thoughts around relationships is crucial.

Jenna became a young female CEO of her family-owned business and sat at the head of the table where men filled most of the other seats inside her organization and in the industry. Her father had created a successful and profitable business and had an established way of doing things. But Jenna needed more freedom in the business moving forward.

At first, Jenna worried about what the employees would think if she changed things. She hesitated to make too many waves in the male-dominated company and field. However, she soon realized that if she didn't just stop worrying about what others thought, she would be trapped in a suffocating and deflating situation.

If you've inherited a business, or you're in a situation where you fear letting go of "the old way of doing things" (even if you're the one who created them!) because others are accustomed to it, give yourself permission to ruffle as many feathers as it takes to move forward into a fresh new vision and completely new territory. It will be exciting, maybe a little scary, but far more fulfilling and freeing than doing the same old thing just because that's "how it's always been done."

Freedom of Brain Power

This is the ultimate freedom. No one gets to tell you what to think, what opinions to have, or how to feel. You get to think about what you want right now and direct your energy and brain power toward what you choose. And ultimately, you get to feel free right now — that feeling is only a choice away.

How you use your brain is your most important freedom because it shapes everything else. When you're choosing how to think and feel about things instead of just reacting, you'll be unstoppable.

Now that you've gained this new kind of freedom let's look at how you'll be able to manage your thoughts around stress. You may be surprised at the results.

THINK BIGGER: FIND YOUR FREEDOM

1. What kinds of freedom do you crave most — time, money, relationships, or brain power? Why?

2. What relationships are restricting or no longer serving you? Why are you holding onto them? If you let go of them, what freedoms would be available to you?

3. If you had these freedoms, what would be possible in your life and business? How would having those possibilities affect your sense of fulfillment?

4. What would Future You tell Present You to do today to start creating more freedom?

CHAPTER 10

BIG FUTURE: A BETTER KIND OF STRESS

Big ideas and big plans are often easier — certainly no more difficult — than small ideas and small plans.

— David J. Schwartz

I've mentioned my client Dominique before. She is a dietician with a specific focus on those suffering from a particular physical disorder. When she came to me, she was totally stressed out. Even though she had established her business and was confident in her craft, she wasn't making any money.

After doing some work, we discovered she was too afraid of putting herself out there or doing business "the wrong way." She kept making excuses that she needed to give herself some time and space to figure this all out. Entrepreneurship was new to her. She never had to take payments, do billing, or start an email marketing campaign. Her lack of the *right* answers to the how-to questions kept her stuck in the same spot.

Her head was like a pinball machine, with thoughts going everywhere. She didn't know what to do with them or where to park them.

One of the classic ways this kind of stress manifests is in passive action, which we've already examined. This is the kind of action that doesn't really require action but feels like action. In Dominique's case, she just kept researching, looking for more knowledge.

Dominique's other issue was that she hadn't started Thinking Big about the impact her practice could have on those families needing her services. She was focused on what wasn't happening instead of what could happen. Paralyzed between two opposing forces — a need for security and a need to take risks and do something more with her business — Dominique ended up doing nothing at all.

She needed to think outside the box about how to grow her business, which had a non-traditional model in her field. Once she decided she had to put things into action and stop sitting on her ideas, she made more connections with other businesses and referral partners and with clients who needed her. She also started feeling more confident talking about what she did, and she perfected her elevator speech.

As her confidence grew, her stress receded. She started to experience stress in a different way, and this shift pushed her to succeed and gave her more confidence even when things didn't work out perfectly right away. She started to enjoy the challenges in her business instead of feeling overwhelmed by and afraid of them.

YES – YOU CAN ENJOY STRESS

One of the most surprising things my clients realize once they change their beliefs and move into their future selves is that though they still have stress, they don't mind it. In fact, they often enjoy it.

I know. You're probably wondering if I've gone off the deep end. But it's true. You can actually look forward to stress — when it's the right kind of stress. Dominique often thanked me for challenging her to make an ask, raise her prices, or tell someone that no, she wasn't driving 100 miles to see a patient — all of which were stressful situations.

If you identify with Dominique's example, the kind of stress you've probably been dealing with is what Jody Moore calls Stuck Stress,[19] which isn't productive. It doesn't take you anywhere; you just move in circles over and over through the same tired thought process.

Stuck Stress narrows your thinking through a lens of fear and anxiety.

The new stress, Progress Stress, doesn't look like that. It doesn't come from the negative feeling of being trapped between two things you want, can't decide on, or don't feel you can achieve. It comes from being excited and curious about something you want to do and being anxious about potentially not reaping the rewards of doing it if you don't get going, which pushes you to make it happen.

This shift comes from all the freedoms you've just realized you have in Chapter 9, which completely change your world. It also comes when you switch from interested to committed. Are you starting to see how all these elements build on each other?

Figure 10.1 Stuck Stress vs. Progress Stress

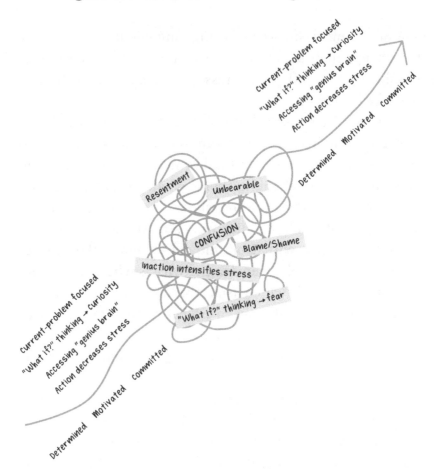

When you start on your journey as an entrepreneur, you may have stress, but it's Progress Stress — full of curiosity, excitement, commitment, and positive energy. Then you get into the "messy middle," where you're not quite sure what your next move is. Stuck Stress takes over, making you confused, afraid, and, well, stuck. As you shift your mindset, you'll get back into Progress Stress.

SEVEN ASSUMPTIONS ABOUT THE FUTURE THAT CREATE STUCK STRESS

Having a vision for your future is supposed to be a positive thing, right? Well, sometimes it's not. When the vision has hidden pitfalls, it will undermine your progress and prevent you from achieving your goals.

We've already looked at how fear sabotages you. However, another obstacle can be attachment. When you're attached to a specific outcome, it can paralyze you or keep you in Stuck Stress. Attachment is what happens when commitment goes too far — and yes, that's possible. Now you're not just all-in — you're all-in with unrealistic expectations.

Here are seven of the most common things clients tell me will happen when they achieve their *perfect reality* — which turns out not to be so perfect.

1. **"Things will be easier when I achieve X."** What this really tells me is the person wants to be free of problems and challenges. But in the last chapter, we learned real freedom isn't freedom from problems and challenges. That's not realistic, and it sets you up for constant disappointment when the world doesn't cooperate with your expectations. When you're constantly disappointed, you're also constantly stressed about the results you're getting. You're battling against reality. That's stressful, and it's not productive.

2. **"I'll be more likable/lovable/desirable when I do/ have/am X."** Deep down, this means the person wants freedom from rejection or hurt. But it's another

one of those externally focused expectations that will lead to disappointment. Defining your value or success based on others' feelings or reactions puts you on a rollercoaster. When someone is upset with you, you often believe it reflects you as a human. You can't expect others' negative or neutral responses won't ever exist. Therefore, using the lack of them as a sign of your success will mean you always feel like you haven't succeeded. That's going to bring you a lot of stuck and unproductive stress.

3. **"I'll finally 'feel legit' when I achieve X."** Expecting to cross some imaginary boundary where you suddenly have the *right amount* of credibility isn't realistic. When you're providing value, people want what you have to offer. If you're delivering a service or a product and people are smiling, then you're as legit as you need to be. When you're constantly evolving and improving, you'll keep learning and getting better, and that's the best you can do. Looking for an imaginary line of legitimacy or a gold star of approval takes away from your satisfaction in the moment and can hamper your ability to serve your clients. If you seek the imaginary line as a sign that you're now valid, you're setting yourself up to feel like you're constantly failing. That feeling will definitely bring you stress, and it's a stress that won't end until you change the belief.

4. **"I'll finally have lots of free time when I achieve X."** Let's get real. What does free time really look like to you? You're a high-achieving, ambitious woman with

extraordinary goals. Do you truly want *free time*, or do you want *the authority to do what you want* with your time? Even if you had free time, how long would it last before you put it toward your goals? All your time should be working to bring you something — even relaxation isn't really free time. It's still serving you. Newsflash: What you really want isn't free time; it's *control over your time.* You learned in Chapter 9 that your time is yours to control. This idea of not having any control over your time or not having enough free time is what created your stress — and not only is that belief unproductive, but so is the stress related to it.

5. **"Things will be perfectly clear when I achieve X. I'll know exactly what I need to do all the time."** Clarity comes from knowing what you want and understanding what you need to do to have it. But expecting pure clarity no matter what is unrealistic. You will still have to think your way through problems and challenges (and remember — when you shift your mindset, you might actually start to like this!). You might get blindsided by unexpected events and reactions from others. That's how life works. If you think your life isn't working because you're not sure what to do, you're being unfair to yourself. Expecting that you'll always know what to do or what ingredients go into the award-winning recipe will create unnecessary stress you can't resolve unless you change the expectation.

6. **"When I achieve X, I'll have so much money in my bank account!"** This is like the "lots of free time"

idea. When you have goals, your money should be working toward those. Often, that means it's not in your bank account (so, remember, the amount in the bank account doesn't tell the whole story) but invested elsewhere — for instance, in your business to hire new team members or to buy new equipment. Or you might invest it to make your home more efficient or to buy a larger home that better suits your family's needs. Or you might just have it invested in the market so it grows. If you have a lot of money in your bank account because you're not doing anything with it to further your success, after a while, you're not going to have any money because you're also not going to have success. That's how this works. It's fine to set aside emergency savings, but that should be something you calculate based on your needs, too. Now that you have a mindset of financial freedom, can you see how your previous worry created unproductive stress? Again — the change of belief is what will get you out, not attaining a number in your bank account.

7. **"Once I get to 'that place,' then I'll be able to hire more people, and everything will be great!"** Really? What is this mythical place you speak of? And what magical creatures will you be hiring that will make your life suddenly so much easier? Remember: Hiring people adds another layer of complexity. They'll expand your capabilities, but they won't necessarily make your life easier. You'll have a whole new set of lessons to learn and challenges to face in managing them. If you expect your life to suddenly get easier,

you're doing not only yourself but them a disservice. It's unrealistic. And like all the other unrealistic expectations I've mentioned, this one will set you up for constant disappointment, too.

EXPERIENCE A DIFFERENT WORLD

When you go through this process and start allowing Future You to breathe freely, you suddenly realize your previous version of success looks nothing like real success. Your previous version of freedom looks nothing like *actual* freedom. And now, you can toss out your previous version of stress because it, too, came from your limiting beliefs and rigid expectations.

In examining what real freedom looks like in Chapter 9, you may have noticed we never talked about freedom being *security*. That's because freedom isn't security. In fact, you can't have real freedom and also have security. You're going to have to give up one or the other. This is a real either/or decision.

Besides, security isn't necessarily a good thing. Too much security can be suffocating. An entrepreneurial soul needs challenge, risk, and exploration. You can't have those and cling to security, too. When you do, guess what? You create Stuck Stress.

When my clients come to me with a problem or challenge and comment on how hard it is, I'm always secretly a little excited for them because I know they're going to get to do some work to free themselves from the burden they are carrying around unnecessarily. And once they tackle the problem and start living up to their potential and creating what they want, every other part of their lives *will* be easier — but not for the reasons they assumed in the Seven Assumptions section. It doesn't get easier because the challenges go away.

It gets easier because doing this work will cause you to experience the world differently. It will cause you to experience yourself differently. It will help you gain confidence. You'll learn to create anything you choose to, differently. It's totally worth doing.

Let me give you a few examples of what could happen.

You deal with difficult people with ease.

One of Lindsey's most important new hires was doing a decent job in most respects, but she was also creating some unnecessary conflict with her behavior. She seemed to have a chip on her shoulder and didn't seem to be giving Lindsey the benefit of the doubt.

At first, Lindsey was daunted by the challenge of handling the situation. But she focused on creating better communication between them and setting behavioral boundaries so she could address those issues objectively and calmly. This situation became a way for Lindsey to expand her leadership skills and learn new ways to deal with difficult situations (and people). As a result, she improved a relationship that was already working in other ways, which meant she didn't have to hire someone else and start all over again.

And this decision also gave Lindsey a type of freedom. Think about what would be more useful — to be easily offended or to be almost never offended? What would serve you better? What would serve your business better? By learning to love people for who they are and not letting them ruffle your feathers, you get to learn from so many people. And that expands your life and world in amazing ways.

You learn to love and embrace yourself and your work.

This is another reason why, when my clients fail at something, I'm secretly excited for them because now they can do some work that will totally change their world. I saw this happening for Carrie.

After operating business #1 for 25 years, Carrie was very used to well-oiled machines. That business was something she could run in her sleep.

But business #2 was new and needed work. She wasn't getting the response she had hoped. Her early morning coffee dates with financial planners weren't bringing in referrals. And the prospective client conversations that did happen did not go smoothly — all too often she heard, "We're just not ready yet," as she virtually sat across from prospective clients at their kitchen tables.

She often became frustrated, shut her computer, and contemplated just giving up on this new idea.

But she stuck with it. She changed her thinking and some of her "new but not working" systems and verbiage. And her Strategic Pause lasted long enough to allow her to notice all she had learned in just a few short months of opening the new business. That realization — all these new skills, new neural pathways — further liberated her. You *can* teach an old dog new tricks!

Ask yourself: Can I love myself no matter what? Do I have my own back? Can I notice my shortcomings, mistakes, and weaknesses and still love me? Can I be there for me? Can I pull myself up by my bootstraps and keep going? Remember: You're either winning or learning.

You have margin in your daily routine to be future-focused.

You have a big goal to accomplish — a financial goal, a business goal, a health goal, even a pleasure goal. And now, since you're no longer stuck in your Past You mindset, you can find time to do the work and go after it.

With a long-term plan and the motivation to achieve it, Lindsey realized she could take action anywhere, at any time. While she waited for her daughter in the car outside gymnastics, she created a job posting for a sales manager as well as signed up for Blue Apron to be delivered next week. Freeing herself from her ridiculous expectations led to finding ways to create more time for important things.

When you choose to actively seek freedom from your day-to-day so you can attend to what you want to attend to, you unlock a part of your brain that helps you achieve that goal without sacrificing your pleasure, productivity, and sanity. You get creative. You trade frustration for curiosity, and you figure it out. And by figuring it out, you gain even more freedom and a few made-for-you delicious meals on the table.

Yes, you have stress while you're figuring it out, but it's Progress Stress, which powers you to move forward and find new solutions. You don't feel hopeless or like a victim. You feel movement and options.

*You give up your rigid expectations and
embrace new opportunities.*

When working with my clients, I often see a pattern that results in Stuck Stress, and it's related to their emotions about the situation.

Remember the "interested versus committed" situation? These are two levels of motivation, but there's also a third — attachment. This is when you go beyond commitment and become attached to a specific process that must be used to achieve the outcome, or you become attached to your expectations of exactly what the outcome must look like. A lot of the time, that attachment relates to your commitments to yourself. So, you have no problem figuring out how to do things for others, but you can't do them for yourself.

For instance, Tamara wanted to start exercising more — spring break was right around the corner. But to her, that immediately meant four days a week at the gym. She was stuck envisioning herself on a treadmill at 6:00 a.m., and since that seemed impossible, she abandoned the goal.

Once she freed herself from those rigid expectations and realized exercising could look like a 20-minute walk around the block with her kids and dog at 5:00 p.m., exercise became an enjoyable, treasured part of every day, and she shed a few pounds too.

Rigid expectations about what you should be doing or how it should look cause you to ghost yourself. Instead of giving yourself time and attention, you dismiss your needs and goals because you've become attached to what the results should look like and how you should achieve them, and thus you've decided they're impossible. However, they're only impossible in the way you see them.

Letting go of the exact process or outcome means taking the ski trip with your daughter, even for just two nights. It means wearing whatever you want to wear, regardless of your age. It means having the holidays and special occasions YOU want to have and deciding that ordering the turkey from Whole Foods is just fine. It means telling people what you want for your birthday. It means setting boundaries and sticking to them; no, the in-laws can't stay with you. It means following through on those passion projects. It means putting your needs first so you can fill your life with peace, joy, freedom, and delight.

You won't necessarily avoid all stress, but your stress won't be due to an attachment to an outcome.

THE HORIZON IS FULL OF NEW DESTINATIONS

Remember when we talked about how managing your time reflects how you're managing your mind? Well, if you've gone through this whole process, you're now managing your time and your mind a lot differently. And it's leading to so many new opportunities you might feel overwhelmed.

Think about that for a minute. Where you were before, you were overwhelmed by your daily routine — so much so that you could barely look up to see where you were or where you wanted to go. You just kept plugging away, trying to get to that elusive place you couldn't even quite describe (let alone believe in). The other day, a client said to me, "I'm putting out fires, but I'm also standing in the fire." That's a great way to put it.

But where are you now? The New You is overwhelmed by new opportunities. Life has become a grand challenge where you see new horizons to explore, and you're already planning your trip to get there. Maybe you see so many different potential destinations that you must sit down and think about what you really want to do because they're all exciting. That's a much different feeling from the Past You.

You may have stress in this situation, but it's not the stress of going in circles or riding in the Fred Flintstone car. It's the result of curiosity, of an excited, "What if this actually happens?" while revving your vehicle's engine before moving confidently out onto the road. External obstacles may exist, but they won't keep you from getting to your destination. They're just bumps in the road, yield signs, or yellow lights, not stop signs or red lights.

You've gotten out of your own way. You're working within your new, ambitious plan, and you've achieved some of those goals. You've realized what true freedom is, and you've conquered negative stress. Now it's time to tackle the next set of challenges that happen when you succeed at your plan. To do that, we'll need to sustain your new mindset to see challenge as fuel for new opportunities. Let's look at that mindset shift that comes with success in the next chapter.

THINK BIGGER: FINESSE YOUR STRESS

1. Think back to the challenge or situation you identified in Chapter 3. Looking at the seven assumptions about Stuck Stress, are any of these assumptions

around that situation preventing you from moving into Progress Stress?

2. What will it take to move into Progress Stress?

3. Have you started Thinking Big as you're reading this book? If so, how?

4. What are the most important things you've realized about yourself during this process? What has surprised you the most about yourself?

CHAPTER 11

BIG OPPORTUNITY: CREATE YOUR NEXT CHALLENGE

Start now. Start where you are.
Start with fear. Start with pain. Start with doubt.
Start with hands shaking.
Start with voice trembling. Just start.

— Sara Blakely (Spanx)

ONE LAST THING

OK, here's the part you've been waiting for. This is the part where Future You, who has achieved a level of success in which everything is easier, wants to tell you this one last thing. After you know it and learn to deal with it, everything is just better. You'll finally start coasting along with your hair whipping in the breeze.

So, here it is.

The one last thing is that there is no One Last Thing.

Once you've accepted that, you'll be much better off.

I know. It's disappointing, isn't it? Just One Last Thing. We'll only have to deal with this negative situation once. Once we figure it all out, we'll be done with it. We'll only have That One Time where we're stuck.

But as we noted in Chapter 9, this expectation leads to more stress. "When X happens, everything will get better" isn't a realistic expectation — and neither is "X will never happen after this."

When you get to a certain point in your plan, and everything is falling into place in one way, it's only going to get challenging in another way because your brain will find a new challenge rooted in your present success. That's how your brain works.

And this is the secret successful businesswomen get. They realize they're never actually going to be finished. There's always another set of challenges that come from solving the ones they're working on now... and that's OK. Even if challenges don't arise in their current businesses, their next set of dreams and ambitions will create new ones.

That's what you've been doing all along — you just didn't think about it in this way. You saw the appearance of new challenges as a negative when in reality, it's just part of your evolution. You're creating your own challenges just as you're solving them. Now, you can embrace the process, with all its ups and downs — and when you do that, you'll experience the world in a completely different way.

You've come full circle, only you're not on a roundabout. The circle is much larger, and you've grown so much since the last time you were here. Big Ben and Parliament don't look the same at all — and neither do you. You're looking at them through the much wiser and differently curious eyes of Future You.

The circle isn't a circle anymore. It's become something else entirely — it's an upward spiral of growth and change. You're not getting nowhere. You're expanding in many new directions all at once around a central focus. Your thinking expands as your knowledge, skill, experience, and confidence expand.

In the spiral, as your business scales up, so do your capabilities and possibilities. You'll keep growing, and so will the spiral — and all the opportunities it brings to you, your family, your community, and your world.

Figure 11.1 The Expanding Spiral of Evolution

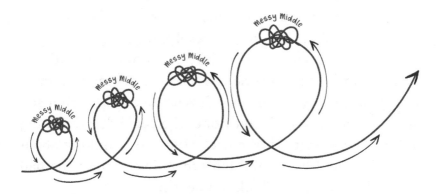

Each time you travel around another bend of the spiral, your knowledge, capabilities, and experience grow. The messy middle is always the same size, but proportionally, it feels smaller and less overwhelming each time.

SUCCESS CAN BE FRUSTRATING... UNTIL IT ISN'T

Here's an example of how a challenge arose from success. One of my clients, Alex, had achieved a successful business in a very niched field as an expert on dinosaurs. She did very well as a solo entrepreneur in a business specializing in educational presentations and exhibits for K–12 schools and other types of organizations. That was all she wanted, and for a while, she felt she had achieved her dream.

However, after a time, Alex grew restless. She started feeling like she wanted to do something more. Her problem was that her current business was so successful she didn't have any time to focus on the next stage of her evolution, which was to become a nationally recognized speaker presenting to larger audiences of science educators. The new role would require her to travel a great deal out of her usual region.

Alex tried to stick it out with her current business, telling herself she was being ungrateful for her success. Yet that very success was now in the way of what she currently wanted. She didn't know how to resolve the problem without giving up her business, which she didn't want to do, either.

After we worked together for a while, she realized most of her problems were in her mind. With an either/or mindset, she assumed she was the only one who could do everything she was doing. Instead, she needed to start thinking about where she could let go and put others in the roles she had been filling so she could take on new ones.

Hiring a team didn't make her life easier, either — at least, not at first. She had to learn how to compensate for travel expenses, manage team benefits, and do other unfamiliar HR-related activities. And would anyone deliver a presentation to a group of 10-year-olds like she did? She had developed this curriculum — it was her baby. Yet facing these fears head-on was worth the time if it allowed her to pursue her next set of dreams while her business was still serving her clients and educating children about something she cared deeply about.

SUCCESS DOESN'T HAVE TO BE A THREAT

All of this goes back to fear of success. We've talked about that in earlier chapters, but now you can see why it exists. There's a grain of truth in it — when you succeed, things can get harder in that you create new challenges for yourself.

The problem is this mindset doesn't factor in that you also learn as you go.

If you succeed at something, you have a whole new set of skills and information to work with when you get to the next thing. You aren't where you were when you started. You're far better prepared to handle the next set of challenges.

So, it's true that when you hire a bunch of people, you're going to have to learn how to manage HR issues, lead a team, and deal with things like travel compensation and benefits... and become a better delegator who trusts. But once you know all of that, you can expand your team as needed without having to learn new skills in those areas. You've already mastered them.

Remember Jenna, who inherited her dad's business? Once she conquered the first hurdle of being a young female CEO of a male-dominated business in a male-dominated industry, her next challenge was becoming more involved in her community and tackling her business challenges from a strategic standpoint. Where did the business need to be in the next 10 years? She now had her employees and leadership team onboard with her, but her true challenges were just beginning. She created the challenges from her own drive and goals. She could have just settled on winning her first battle and then going back to the status quo for the rest of the business, but she wanted more.

LIFE: THE MOVIE

When my clients complain about a particular situation being tough or not what they expected, I tell them to think about it like they're in a movie.

"Pretend you're watching a movie on the big screen in a theater. This is the part of the movie where the tough things happen, and the heroine has to figure it out," I say. "Or maybe this is the happy part where everything goes great." Movies aren't all rainbows and daisies. Only some parts are; that's what makes them great. Good movies evoke a range of emotions.

While the element of humor there helps bring things into better perspective, it also helps the person get some distance from themselves. Seeing your life from the perspective of a movie-goer lets you step back and not be so attached to outcomes or situations. You get to decide what to do to change the trajectory of the movie. You get to choose how you create the next scene. What action will you take?

You can take it a step further and start analyzing the movie. What genre movie is it? Drama? Comedy? Adventure?

Documentary? Do you like that genre? Why? Why not? Can you change it to one you do like?

You get to determine the movie ending — but keep in mind there will always be a new movie. As soon as one story ends, another will begin. Your life is really a series of movies. Each major challenge is its own movie. When the series ends, it will be because your life ends. So, enjoy your movies while you can, and make the most of them. You're the heroine, after all. Do you want to be a victim or a strong, courageous fighter? I already know the answer to that question.

If you want to hear more about this movie technique, check out my podcast *Time to Level Up*, Episode 72, "Live Life Like a Movie."[20]

GO BEYOND EITHER/OR

Past You, who was overwhelmed and dreading the next problem that could arrive on her doorstep, didn't know how to handle the next set of challenges. But the Future You does.

You have a plan. Does that mean the world will work according to it? Probably not. So, you already know you're going to face setbacks and situations you didn't anticipate. However, unlike Past You, New You, the Extraordinary Achiever, is tuned into the future and knows what Future You would do.

Past You believed a lot of things *had to* be a certain way, or else you weren't a success. Future You knows you're either winning or learning. You're never a failure with that mindset. You're just a work in progress, like everyone else.

Past You used simplistic judgment, labeling everything as either "good" or "bad" and any kind of conflict or stress bad. Future You realizes that sometimes things are good AND bad at the same time. For instance, hiring people is good and bad. It creates more conflict, stress, and complexity but may be necessary to solve specific capacity problems. In some situations, it may not be the right answer. But in others, it's worth taking on the challenge.

An expectation that things should always be good isn't realistic. Life is 50/50; it's not all about positive thoughts and positive experiences. Polly Positive is just as bad as your Frenemy, just in a different way. Trying to have only a positive, perfect life can be toxic for you and everyone else. Yes, there is such a thing as "toxic positivity."

Think of it like this: Everything won't be rainbows and unicorns just because you're on vacation. Kids will fight. You might go to a crappy restaurant. It may rain. If these things happen, are you going to let them ruin your whole vacation?

On the other hand, "There's a possibility it *might* rain on vacation, and that's OK" is a useful thought. You can make plans for potential rain versus expecting, "It's always going to be sunny," and then being disappointed when the weather doesn't cooperate.

Life is like that. Half the time will be great, and half the time won't. If you plan for the times it won't, your reaction will be totally different. Instead of disappointment and resentment, you'll just say, "Oh, this part is one of those not-great parts. This is the part of my movie where I get to experience disappointment, and that's OK." And then you'll go about your business instead of wasting energy being angry.

The either/or, good or bad rule applies to people, too. Every situation doesn't need to have a victim and a villain. You can be both right and wrong at the same time, and so can the other person. Future You realizes things are complex and not so black and white. And when you get out of the good/bad thinking, you realize how limiting it was.

As they reach this realization, my clients invariably tell me some version of the same thing.

"How do you feel?" I ask.

"Relieved," they say at first.

It is a relief. Because the "right/wrong" mentality is a huge source of Stuck Stress. It keeps you paralyzed from moving toward opportunity.

But relief is only a short-term change of feeling from realizing something isn't bad like you thought it was. Over the long term, they have a different answer.

"I feel like I have power," they tell me.

Empowerment is a long-term answer. Suddenly, there's not a right and wrong way to do everything. Each situation has multiple right ways. They can make lemonade out of lemons.

It's OK for Alex to let go of her daily roles so others can take on those responsibilities. Doing that isn't wrong, and she doesn't have to focus on her current business OR her new one — she can have both.

Jenna's dad's version of running their family business was *right* in some ways and *wrong* in others; her version will be, too — but not in the *same* ways. In this new perspective, she no longer gravitates back and forth between two impossible scenarios. She's able to be comfortable with the new version of right and continues to improve it as she sees fit.

Future You can take on any challenge, confident that you'll find your own version of the right and wrong way to do it, and you'll win and learn along the way.

THINK BIGGER: GO FROM "EITHER/OR" TO "AND"

1. Write down five things you have either/or beliefs about. For example:

   • "Marriage is good."
   • "Being single is bad."
   • "Always being there for my friends is good."
   • "Taking time for myself is bad."

2. Now, for each, restate it with AND.

   • "Marriage is good and bad."
   • "Being single is good and bad."
   • "Always being there for my friends is good and bad."
   • "Taking time for myself is good and bad."

3. What needs to happen for you to believe the AND statements? What new thoughts will you have to borrow from?

4. How will shifting to AND statements change your outcome?

CHAPTER 12

BIG WORK:
THE WORK
WORTH DOING

There is no problem outside of you that is superior to the power within you.

— **Bob Proctor**

*I*n *The Alchemist*, Paulo Coelho tells a story about a young man named Santiago who has a recurring dream while lying under a tree by a church. The dream gives him a vision of a treasure buried under the Great Pyramids in Egypt. The Pyramids are far away from the man's home, but he decides to set out on a journey to find the treasure. He encounters several alchemists along the way, and while he learns lessons from them, he also runs into a lot of trouble. Along the way, he encounters several temptations to end his journey prematurely, but he continues. With the last alchemist's teaching, he also gains the powers of an alchemist.

He finally makes it all the way to Egypt and starts digging for the treasure, only to have men accost him and beat him. When they learn he's digging for treasure, they decide he must not have any money. But when they learn he's doing it because of a dream, one of them scoffs, telling him dreams have no power. The man tells Santiago he himself has been dreaming of a treasure, only it's located under a sycamore tree by a church. This is the very tree Santiago had his dream under!

So, Santiago heads back to his home, but he now has the power of an alchemist, as well as a wife-to-be waiting for him, all gained on his adventure. And the treasure still waits back home.

PARTING THOUGHTS

Well, my friend, we've reached the end of our journey together — at least, the journey in this book.

This has been a journey through your mind, heart, and soul. And I hope you've enjoyed making it.

As you've been reading, I hope you've also been doing the work. But if not, I hope you'll go back now and complete the exercises and questions in the Think Bigger sections at the end of each chapter. Because it really is the work worth doing.

Like Santiago, when you "return home," you will not be the same person. You will have gained power, knowledge, and insight. And you'll even have a treasure you didn't know you had waiting for you.

That treasure is you.

But that's how it's supposed to be. Remember? Being an entrepreneur is a journey in personal development disguised as an entrepreneurial adventure. With the end of this book, your adventure is just beginning.

As I've noted, most of this work — even the planning you just did — has revolved around changing your mindset. What you've done is move further along on a journey to become the next best version of yourself — to live up to your potential. This is the Strategic Pause you needed to catch your breath and decide who you are and what you're really trying to do.

"Work worth doing" is work that happens first in your head and heart. It's learning who you're being and becoming and what you're feeling. It's often harder than any external action. But it brings you to the next level — the level of inspired action and Extraordinary Achievement.

As I've shown, when you've done the work to know yourself, you can change your world. That means your world gets better, which is the result you want. But what does that mean in the bigger picture?

It means you're not constantly feeling like a disappointment, a failure, or a jumble of confusion. In giving more thought and time to yourself, you've empowered yourself to give more to your family, your clients, your colleagues, and your community — and whomever else you choose. Most of all, you're giving more to the Future You, and that's an investment you'll see a return on through the rest of your life.

Anything can move from feeling impossible or out of reach to feeling inevitable and your reality. It's a matter of changing your thinking and shifting from the "no way" constricting/restricting to the "of course" curious/freeing approach in life.

You can go beyond and live an extraordinary life that is so enthralling you want to participate. The only thing that can stop you is you — not the external forces you want to blame. The key is being willing to experience all the feelings that go along with it.

THINK BIGGER: YOU'RE WORTH IT

1. For more on why this process is so important, listen to my podcast, *Time to Level Up* — specifically episode 96, "The Difference Between Doing Work and Doing the Work That's Worth Doing."

2. What would your life and business look and feel like if you started Thinking Big today? What would be possible that today seems impossible?

3. Who is on your "Board of Directors"? Who supports you in your quest for growth? Do you need some new members to fill the seats?

4. Don't forget to download more resources from my website at **AndreaLiebross.com/toolkit** if you haven't already done so.

5. Connect with me via my website, social or email (all of that is on the About the Author page). I believe in you more right now than you believe in yourself. Going it

alone is hard. And even if you're not physically alone, you most likely are alone in your thoughts. You're stuck in your own peanut butter jar, and I'm here to help you read the label. Let's do this!

ACKNOWLEDGMENTS

Writing this book and translating my thoughts into words has been an amazing undertaking and something I thought I would never do until I believed I could do it. Writing a book was for *other people*; I'm more of a talker. So, to see words on a page inside a book with my own name on the cover is really living out my Future You.

This book wouldn't have come to fruition without the incredible support team I have in place. This is a short list of the many people who have helped make this book possible — who have held my belief alongside me, helped me make decisions, create a plan, and put it into action.

I'll start by thanking the Niche Pressworks team, especially Nicole Gebhardt, who told me at a McAlister's Deli in Indianapolis about 10 years ago that I should write a book. I specifically remember telling her I wasn't ready. Little did I know writing a book is kind of like having a baby: You're never really ready.

Thank you also to her team, Kim Han and Nadia Belcher, and for introducing me to Michael Hague, a master storyteller, who was able to pull my own story out of me in less than 60 minutes. I also owe a big, extraordinary thanks to my editing team: Ellen Polk, for catching all the details that needed to be attended to, and Melanie Hahn-Greene, without whom I couldn't have completed this book, literally and figuratively. Thank you for your honesty, kindness, and laughs along the way as we created this masterpiece together.

I owe many thanks to my photographer, Kim Beesley, who continues to be able to capture my personality through photography. Not only are you a great friend, but you're a master at your craft and have taught me how to pick apart photos like no one else.

Thank you to Deena Rutter for helping create incredible graphics, Tami Boyce for the fabulous cover design, and Suzanne T. Moore for crafting my web pages and giving me incredible insight on promotion.

Thank you to Lynda Carlini, my online business manager by title, but also my friend, supporter, believer, and reality checker. She helps make my business run, top to bottom, and I couldn't be doing what I'm doing today without her.

Thank you to my coach, Stacey Hylen, who is always just a Voxer away, for supporting me in this quest and for encouraging me to finally pull the trigger and write the book.

Thank you to my friends near and far, who are always there to listen and offer words of encouragement even when they can't quite figure out what I'm doing and why.

And thank you to my parents. My father, Frank, has been my real-life example of entrepreneurship. I have watched him from the time I was five and continue to watch him grow his own business (even at age 85), serve his clients, manage his employees, and work hard, especially during tax season. Thank you to my mom, Mary, who has shown me what it means to be kind and to love unconditionally from day one.

Thank you to my children, to Brett, my firstborn who never gives up, goes after what he wants 100 percent, and is one of my biggest cheerleaders, and to my daughter Rebecca who serves as my example of what it is like to be a young woman in today's world, and whose wit and blatant honesty I appreciate in all things — from clothes to makeup to social media posts.

And a huge thanks to my husband Rob, who has supported me with unwavering love, not just in this endeavor of writing a book, but in all my endeavors over the years. He is the definition of supportive. His patience is incredible.

And finally, thank you to all my clients for opening up, trusting me, and sharing your stories with me as you give me insight into how we evolve. You're my real research lab. I find extraordinary joy in supporting you in all facets of life. Your wins are wins for me, too.

*A*ndrea Liebross is a coach, speaker, and host of the *Time to Level Up* podcast. She's known for helping high-achieving entrepreneurial women make the shift from overwhelm to freedom so they stop thinking small and start thinking big. Through her work, she guides bold, ambitious women to create their own secret sauce for success by combining two ingredients: the right mindset and solid systems.

Andrea shows women how to shift from believing what they want is impossible, complex, and daunting to possible just by simplifying, making things doable and FUN (even the systems), and adding a bit of confidence. Andrea's signature process leads them to find success on their OWN terms and, ultimately, to joy and freedom in life and business.

After graduating from Dartmouth College and marrying the guy who lived down the hall, Andrea and her husband moved from the Northeast (go Red Sox) and settled in Indianapolis. Over the last few decades, Andrea started three successful businesses and became a certified business and life coach, all while raising two kids (at the time of writing, ages 22 and 19) and two giant Leonbergers (they might be more work than the kids!).

Andrea is available for coaching, speaking engagements, and workshops. Connect with her here:

🌐 AndreaLiebross.com

🎙 Time To Level Up

ⓕ @AndreaLiebrossCoaching

📷 @Andrea.Liebross.Coaching

in @Andrea-Liebross

▶ @AndreaLiebrossCoaching

DOWNLOAD YOUR

THINK *big* TOOLKIT

For MUST-HAVE planning tools that work seamlessly with the book to help you **stop overthinking and make confident, quick decisions to get what you want — every single time,** download my Think Big Toolkit. (I couldn't fit everything in the book!)

AndreaLiebross.com/toolkit

I look forward to hearing your success stories!

WANT HELP THINKING **BIG**, PLANNING **BIG**, AND GETTING **BIG** RESULTS?

The book is a great starting tool, but a coach can help you put it all into action. **If you want a co-pilot on speed dial** to get you on the right track fast, let's work together!

I offer a variety of ever-changing coaching opportunities, including workshops, groups, and private coaching. I'm also happy to come and speak to your team. You can find the latest options on my website:

AndreaLiebross.com

I can't wait to meet you!

P.S. Don't forget to check out my podcast, Time to Level Up, for ongoing motivation and tips for creating the life and business you've always dreamed of. Subscribe via your podcast app, or here: ***AndreaLiebross.com/podcast***

ENDNOTES

1   GEM (Global Entrepreneurship Monitor), *Global Entrepreneurship Monitor 2022/2023 Global Report: Adapting to a "New Normal."* (London: GEM, 2023).
2   Brooke Castillo, "Episode 16: Massive Action," The Life Coach School, July 31, 2014, https://thelifecoachschool.com/podcast/16/.
3   Douglas J. Lisle and Alan Goldhamer, *The Pleasure Trap: Mastering the Hidden Force that Undermines Health & Happiness,* (Encinitas, CA: Healthy Living Publications, April 2006).
4   James Hayton and Gabriella Cacciotti, "How Fear Helps (and Hurts) Entrepreneurs," *Harvard Business Review,* April 03, 2018, https://hbr.org/2018/04/how-fear-helps-and-hurts-entrepreneurs.
5   Michael Hyatt, "6 Steps to Trade Limiting Beliefs for Liberating Truths," *Full Focus,* October 10, 2022, https://fullfocus.co/6-steps-to-trade-limiting-beliefs-for-liberating-truths/
6   Michael Hyatt, "6 Steps."
7   Chevy Chase as Clark Griswald, *National Lampoon's European Vacation,* directed by Amy Heckerling (1985; Burbank, CA: Warner Bros.).

8   Brooke Castillo, "Organize Your Mind," *Life Coach School Podcasts,* Episode 184, https://thelifecoachschool. com/podcast/184/#transcript.

9   Mike Krupit, "The Most Common Beliefs of Entrepreneurs and How to Overcome Them," Trajectify, September 8, 2021, https://www.trajectify.com/blog/ common-limiting-beliefs.

10 Product Plan, "Eisenhower Matrix," accessed April 11, 2023, https://www.productplan.com/glossary/ei senhowermatrix/#:~:text=President%20Dwight%20 Eisenhower%20himself%20developed,president%20 of%20the%20United%20States.

11 Jim Collins and Jerry I. Porras, *Built to Last: Successful Habits of Visionary Companies* (New York: HarperCollins, 2002).

12 Stacy Boehman, "Belief Plans," *Make Money as a Life Coach,* https://staceyboehman.com/belief-plans/.

13 Gino Wickman, *Traction: Get a Grip on Your Business* (Dallas, TX: BenBella Books, 2011).

14 *Cambridge Dictionary,* s.v. "priority," accessed April 15, 2023, https://dictionary.cambridge.org/us/dictionary/ english/priority.

15 Michael Hyatt, "How to Set Goals You'll Actually Achieve," Full Focus, accessed April 15, 2023, https:// fullfocus.co/ how-to-set-goals-youll-actually-achieve/.

16 Michael Hyatt, *Free to Focus: A Total Productivity System to Achieve More by Doing Less,* Chapter 2 (Baker Books, 2019).

17 Bri Fairley, "Ten Principles of Neuroplasticity," Atlas Aphasia Center, accessed February 28, 2023, https://www. atlasaphasia.org/post/10-principles-of-neuroplasticity.

18 John Olivant, The Four Entrepreneurial Freedoms,
    February 13, 2019, https://www.johnolivant.
    com/2019/02/13/.

19 Taken from concepts by Jody Moore, Be Bold webinar,
    December 2021.

20 Andrea Liebross, "Living Life Like a Movie," *Time
    to Level Up*, Episode 72, April 5, 2022, https://
    AndreaLiebross.com/Living-Life-Like-a-Movie/.

Made in the USA
Las Vegas, NV
26 September 2023